Candle
Bedtime Bible

Published by Candle Books
an imprint of
Lion Hudson plc
Wilkinson House, Jordan Hill Road,
Oxford OX2 8DR, England
www.lionhudson.com/candle

ISBN 978 1 85985 955 1
e-ISBN 978 1 78128 090 4

First edition 2013

Acknowledgments
The Lord's Prayer on page 120 is adapted from the Good News Bible
© 1994 published by the Bible Societies/HarperCollins Publishers Ltd UK,
Good News Bible © American Bible Society 1966, 1971, 1976, 1992.
Used with permission.

A catalogue record for this book is available from the British Library

Printed and bound in Singapore, July 2013, LH01

Candle Bedtime Bible

Three, Five and Ten-Minute Stories

Written by Karen Williamson
Illustrated by Christine Tappin

CANDLE
BOOKS

This book is made up of 3, 5, and 10-minute stories.
The colour of the clock face indicates the length of the story.

Contents

At the Very Beginning

IN THE VERY BEGINNING, God made heaven and earth. There were no people. No animals. No life.

And there was no light. It was dark. Very dark. *Completely* dark.

So on the first day God said, "Let there be light!" And there was light.

We call the light "day" and the darkness "night". And God saw it was good. That was on day one!

On day two God put water in the sea and clouds in the sky. And God saw it was good. That was it for day two!

A green earth

Then on day three God was very busy. He made dry land – mountains, hills, and valleys. After this he made oceans, seas, and lakes; rivers, waterfalls, and streams.

After he'd done this, God said, "Now let the earth turn green. Let grass, flowers, and trees grow. Let them all have seeds and fruit!"

At once lush grass, bright flowers, and tall trees started to grow on the earth. There were so many different sorts of grasses, flowers, and trees that nobody could count them all.

And God saw that it was good. All good. That is what happened on day three.

Then on day four God said, "There should be lights in the sky! They will help divide up time into hours, days, months, and years."

And God saw it was good. All *very* good. That was day five!

Then on day six God said, "Let there be life on the earth!"

So on day six he created all the creatures that live on land. He made dogs and cows, horses and camels, lions and bears, lizards and mice, worms and snails – and many, many more. Beetles and worms, elephants and alligators, wombats and ostriches, flamingoes and badgers.

And God saw that it was good. All very good. But still he thought something was missing. There were no people!

The seasons

So God made spring and summer, harvest time and winter. He made the sun to warm the earth in the daytime.

God saw that the night was very dark, so he put the moon and the stars in the sky. That same night the moon and stars came out for the first time.

And that was day four's work finished! *Phew!* It was all good.

On day five God said, "Let there be living creatures in the water – and in the air!"

So he made fish and all the other creatures that swim in water: jellyfish, eels, sharks, whales, and turtles. Shellfish, flying fish, flat fish, luminous fish, crabs, lobsters, and seahorses.

And God made birds and all the other flying creatures. He made eagles that soar, hawks that swoop, and hummingbirds that dart. He made larks that sing and owls that hoot. He made every shape and size of bird.

Adam and Eve

So God said, "Now I shall create humans."

Then God created the first man, Adam, and the first woman, Eve. God made them like himself. He made them so they could be his friends.

God said to Adam and Eve: "Start a family. Let your family spread out all over the earth! It will be your job to care for the fish, the birds, and all the other creatures."

After he created the first humans, God looked at everything he had made.

It was all very good.

So on day seven God rested! He said: "I have finished what had to be done."

And that's how God created the heavens and the earth.

Genesis chapters 1–2

Adam and Eve Leave the Garden

GOD GAVE ADAM AND EVE a beautiful garden called Eden. They were free to live there.

"Now you can give names to all the animals I have created," God told them.

What fun Adam and Eve had, making up names for all the living creatures! Alligators and caterpillars, hippopotamuses and tortoises, squirrels and porpoises.

"Enjoy the garden," God said to Adam. "You can eat anything you like here."

But God gave Adam and Eve a special warning. "*Never, ever* eat the fruit from that special tree in the middle of the Garden of Eden," he told them.

So Adam and Eve started to explore the beautiful garden. They enjoyed the flowers and fruit, they sat by the streams and lakes. They walked through the clusters of trees and lay in the soft grass.

And Adam and Eve looked after all the creatures that were living peaceably with them in the Garden of Eden.

11

A slithery visitor

One day a sneaky snake slithered up to Eve.

"Sssssss," he sneered. "Why don't you steal a bite from the fruit on *that* tree?"

"But that's the fruit God told us never to eat," said Eve.

"Sssssss," hissed the snake again. "Just take one teeny, tiny bite. It surely can't matter."

So Eve took a bite of the fruit on the forbidden tree.

Before long Adam came to find her.

"Here, taste this fruit," said Eve. "I've had a bite – and it hasn't hurt me."

She gave some to Adam. And he too bit into the forbidden fruit.

That same afternoon God came walking in the Garden of Eden. Adam and Eve hid behind some trees.

"Adam! Eve! Where are you?" God called.

When he found them he asked: "Why are you hiding away from me?"

"Eve gave me *that* fruit – so I ate it," said Adam.

"The tricksy snake tempted me," said Eve, trying to blame someone else too. "That's why I ate the fruit."

God was very sad. Adam and Eve had not done as he had told them. They had disobeyed him. So God sent them both out of the beautiful garden.

Forever.

Hard work

God told angels with flashing swords to stop Adam and Eve returning to the Garden of Eden. Never again would they see its beautiful flowers and tall trees, or enjoy quiet walks beside its peaceful rivers.

Adam and Eve felt very sorry and very sad. Outside the garden, they had to work so hard. Now Adam and Eve had to grow all their own food.

The ground was hard and rough. Weeds and thistles grew everywhere. Adam and Eve worked on the land day after day. Digging and sowing, hoeing and raking, weeding and watering. Hard, tiring work.

They often remembered the happy times when they still lived in the Garden of Eden.

Genesis chapters 2–3

Noah Builds a Great Ark

ADAM AND EVE had two sons, named Cain and Abel. In time, Cain and Abel had children too. And before long, hundreds of people were living on the earth.

But it soon became a bad world. People were hurting one another. Stealing from one another. Lying to each other. Fighting with one another. Killing one another.

God began to feel sorry he had ever created the earth and its people. But he saw there was still one good man living on the earth. His name was Noah.

One day God spoke to Noah. "Listen! I'm going to send a great flood," God told him. "I will cover the whole earth with water. There will be nowhere to hide. Then, when the flood is over, I'll give the world a fresh start."

Noah was very worried. "How can I save my family from this terrible flood?" he asked God fearfully.

A special plan

"I've made a special plan to save you and your family," God told Noah. "You must build yourself a huge ship – the biggest anyone has ever made." God thought a moment. "Let's call it your *ark*."

"I'll do exactly what you tell me," said Noah.

He was so glad his family would be safe.

God explained to Noah exactly how to build this great ark. What size it should be. How many doors. How many windows. How to make sure water didn't leak in.

Noah's ark had to be very strong, because floodwater would smash against it.

Noah and his family began to build the ark. Noah's three sons – Shem, Ham, and Japheth – all helped. They cut down trees. They sawed planks of wood. They hammered and planed, waterproofed and painted. They worked for month after month, because this ship would be the biggest ever built. It was three floors high, with lots of big rooms inside. But it had just one door and just one window.

Very curious

Some of the people living nearby watched curiously. "Why ever are you building a ship on dry land?" they asked Noah. "Have you gone quite mad?"

"Soon great floods will come," Noah explained. "Water will cover the earth. But we're going inside our ark. We'll float safely on the water. We will all be very safe."

"What nonsense! Fancy believing such stuff," people scoffed. "You must be out of your mind!"

But Noah wasn't put off. He and his sons – Shem, Ham, and Japheth – just went on sawing and hammering.

Then God gave Noah another important instruction: "Collect up two of every kind of animal."

So Noah and his sons – Shem, Ham, and Japheth – collected two of every creature on earth. Two fierce lions, two howling tigers, two polar bears, two lumbering elephants, two scuttling lice, two cawing ravens, two cooing doves – even two spinning spiders and two scarlet ladybirds. All of them would be saved from the flood that was coming.

When at last the ark was finished, the weather changed suddenly. The skies grew darker. The sun hid. A fierce wind howled.

"The great flood is on its way," Noah told his family. "It's time to enter the ark."

Into the ark

So Noah opened the door of the ark. He and his sons led all the creatures into the great ship, two by two. Two fierce lions, two howling tigers, two polar bears, two lumbering elephants, two scuttling lice, two cawing ravens, two cooing doves – even two spinning spiders and two scarlet ladybirds.

Then God told Noah, "Now you must climb inside the ark too, taking your wife, your sons – Shem, Ham, and Japheth – and their wives."

Noah and his family went inside. And God shut the great door. *Crasshhh!*

The dove returns

Slowly, slowly, the waters went down. Then one day the ark came to rest, with a mighty roar and a crash. They were no longer afloat! The ark was resting on firm ground again.

"I'm going to send out a raven," Noah told his family. "It will fly out, over the water." The raven flapped its wings and flew away from the ark. It went back and forth, waiting for the water to dry up.

After this, Noah sent a dove. But she soon flew back: the dove could find nowhere to perch and rest. Noah knew there wasn't yet much land above water.

A week later, Noah sent out the dove again. Once more she flew back to the ark. But this time the little dove was carrying a fresh, green leaf in her beak. Everyone smiled happily. It meant the tops of trees were now above water.

Noah sent out the dove a third time. This time she never came back. Noah knew that at last the floods had gone. It was time for everyone to leave the ark.

The great door was opened. Noah, his family, and all the creatures left the ark. The fierce lions, the howling tigers, the polar bears, the lumbering elephants, the scuttling lice, the cawing ravens, the cooing doves – even the spinning spiders and the scarlet ladybirds – all came out of the ark.

The animals ran off to find food. All the

The wind howled and shook the ark. Lightning flashed, thunder rumbled. Rain started to fall. Harder and harder it rained. The water began to rise. Before long, water covered the land and everything growing on it.

The ark began to rock. Then the water lifted the ark off the ground. It floated high in the water.

Soon Noah and his family got used to the rain hammering on the roof of the ark and the roar of thunder. The animals had to be fed and watered. There were lots of jobs to be done.

For forty days and forty nights Noah, his family, and all the creatures stayed safe inside the ark.

Then at last the wind began to drop. Gradually the rain stopped. The birds started to flutter their wings. Soon it would be safe to fly in the sky once more.

birds flew away, high into the air.

Noah and his family were so happy. They thanked God for keeping them safe.

A promise

Then God made a special promise. "Never again will a great flood cover the earth," God said solemnly. "As long as the earth remains, there will be seed time and harvest, summer and winter. I am placing a wonderful rainbow in the clouds. Whenever you see it, remember my promise."

When it rains, often we see the rainbow. It reminds us of the story of Noah, and how he was saved from the flood that covered the earth.

Genesis chapters 6:9 – 9:17

Abram Makes a Fresh Start

LONG, LONG AGO, in a far-off land called Ur, there lived a man named Abram. He was married to Sarah. Abram and Sarah were both old, but they had no children.

One day God said to Abram, "Leave home! Leave everything behind: your house, your friends, and your relations. Take a long journey to a new country. Because I am going to give you a special new land."

Abram and Sarah were brave. They believed God – and they were both ready to leave home. They packed their bags and

loaded their animals. Then they set out, taking with them their servants, their camels, their cattle, and their sheep.

Abram had no map for their journey. But God told him, "I will show you where to go – and how to reach the land I have promised you."

A new land

After journeying for many, many months, Abram and Sarah came at last to the land that God had promised. It was called Canaan. In this country there were lush, green valleys and fast-flowing rivers.

"This is the country I told you about!" God said to Abram. "I'm giving this land to you, to your children, and to your grandchildren."

Abram had brought with him his nephew Lot. But Lot kept picking arguments with Abram. Lot wanted to have all the best land for *his* sheep to graze on.

Finally Abram tired of all the quarrels. "All right, Lot – you can have the best land," Abram offered generously.

Now Abram and Sarah settled down to live in their new land – their new home. Abram thanked God for bringing him to such a wonderful country.

Abram soon became very rich. His flocks of sheep grew larger and larger, and his herds of camels bigger and bigger. But Abram always remembered God's promise: "One day you will have many children, grandchildren, and great-grandchildren."

"Count the stars!"

By now Sarah was too old to have children. Abram was even older. And still Abram and Sarah had neither a son nor a daughter.

"We've been waiting many years to start a family," Abram complained to God. "Are we both to die before we have any children?"

Then one night God spoke to Abram. "Step outside your tent," he told him.

So Abram stood under the night sky.

"Look at all those stars!" said God.

Abram looked up.

"Can you count them?" God asked.

Abram shook his head.

"You will have just as many children, grandchildren, and great-grandchildren as there are stars in the sky," God promised. "They will be as many as the grains of sand on the seashore. You just wouldn't be able to count them."

Abram believed what God told him. It was his ninety-ninth birthday! To mark it, God changed his name to "Abraham" – which means "father of many".

The three visitors

Not long after, Abraham was sitting in the shade in front of his tent one day. It was lunchtime, and the sun was burning down. Suddenly, along came three men he'd never seen before.

"Come and sit in the shade with me," Abraham called to the strangers. "It's cooler here – and you can eat with me."

"Quick! Can you bake some bread?"

Abraham asked Sarah.

"Prepare a feast!" he told his servant.

When lunch was ready, Abraham brought it out to his visitors. They sat down to eat and drink together. After the meal, one of the strangers asked Abraham, "Where's your wife, Sarah?"

"She's inside the tent," Abraham answered.

"Next year Sarah is going to have a baby," the visitor told him. "A baby boy."

Laughter

Sarah was listening through the wall of the tent. She laughed! She heard what the stranger said – but she didn't believe a word of it.

"We're *much* too old for that to happen," she said to herself. "I can't possibly have children at my age."

"Why did Sarah laugh?" the stranger asked Abraham. "*Nothing* is impossible for God."

And sure enough, about a year later, Sarah had a baby boy – just as God had promised.

Sarah was so happy. "God has made me laugh," she said. "And everyone who hears about this will want to laugh with me."

So Sarah named her baby Isaac, which means "laughter".

Genesis chapters 12–18

A Wife for Isaac

LITTLE ISAAC GREW UP to be a fine young man. He helped his old father, Abraham, look after his flocks of sheep and herds of cattle.

The day came when Abraham and Sarah thought it was time for Isaac to get married.

Abraham called for his trusted servant, Eliezer. "Go back to the land I came from," Abraham told him. "There you must find a good wife for my son Isaac."

So Abraham's servant loaded up his camels with rich gifts and set out on the long, dusty journey to find a wife for young Isaac.

Eliezer's problem

At last Eliezer arrived in the country Abraham came from. But he suddenly realized he had a problem. "I've no idea *how* to find a wife for Isaac!" he thought. "How will I know when I've found the right woman?"

Eliezer stopped, climbed down from his camel, and sat by a well to think it over.

As he was sitting there, God told him, "The woman who gives water for your camels to drink will be Isaac's wife."

Not long after, a beautiful young woman came to the well to fetch water. On her head, she was carrying a water pot.

"Sir, would you like me to draw water from the well for your camels?" the young woman asked Abraham's servant politely. "You look as if you've come a long way – your camels must be thirsty."

At once Eliezer knew this must be the woman God wanted to be Isaac's wife.

Water for the camels

Watering the camels was not a quick job. Thirsty camels drink lots of water. And these camels had just finished a long journey across the desert, with little to drink on the way. Backwards and forwards the young woman hurried, pouring water for all Eliezer's camels.

"May I ask your name?" Abraham's servant asked her.

"I'm called Rebekah," she told him. "You are a stranger here. Come home and meet my family. You can stay with us."

So Abraham's servant followed Rebekah home to meet her family. When he arrived, Eliezer took out the gifts he had brought with him and gave them to her family.

Eliezer's request

"I've come on a special errand for my master, Abraham," Eliezer told Rebekah's father. "I am seeking a wife for his young son, Isaac. Will you allow your beautiful daughter Rebekah to marry Abraham's son?"

Rebekah's father thought over what Eliezer had asked. Then he spoke.

"Yes," said Rebekah's father. "I would be delighted to give my daughter to be Isaac's wife."

So Rebekah packed her things and set off for the Promised Land with Abraham's servant, Eliezer.

The camels swayed and bumped along the road to the Promised Land of Canaan, where Isaac lived with his parents, Abraham and Sarah. The journey lasted many days.

How Rebekah looked forward to meeting the man she was to marry!

One evening, just before sunset, the camels halted. A young man was walking in the fields. He looked up and saw the camels.

It was Isaac! He saw the beautiful young woman riding on one of the camels. His bride had come! Isaac loved Rebekah very much – and married her.

Genesis chapter 24

Troublesome Twins

ISAAC AND REBEKAH were soon happily married. At first Rebekah had no children. Both of them dearly wanted to have a family. And they knew the promise God had made to Abraham years before: "One day you will have as many children, grandchildren, and great-grandchildren as there are stars in the night sky." So Isaac and Rebekah prayed to God. After that, it wasn't long before Rebekah was expecting a baby.

When the time came for Rebekah to give birth, she discovered she had twins – twin boys. The firstborn twin was red and very hairy, even when he was a baby. His proud parents named him Esau. But Jacob, the second twin baby, was quite different. Jacob had soft, smooth skin.

As they grew up, the twin brothers became less and less like each other. They looked different, they did different things. They didn't even get on well together.

Esau, the older brother, was bold and fearless. He loved to go out hunting for wild animals. He was a real adventurer. Jacob was quite different. He liked to stay at home with his mother, Rebekah, who loved him more than Esau. And Jacob was always full of tricks.

Jacob tricks his brother

One day Esau came home tired from hunting. He'd been stalking animals under the hot sun all day, and he felt very hungry. He noticed Jacob was cooking some delicious broth in a pot.

"I'm starving!" said Esau. "Give me some of your broth! I'm dying for something to eat!"

As we know, Jacob was always up to tricks. Thinking quickly, he said to his brother Esau, "Give me your special rights as Isaac's oldest son – and you can have as much broth as you want!"

"All right," said Esau foolishly. "It's a deal! I'm so hungry, I'd give anything to get some food inside me."

So Jacob gave Esau a steaming bowl of broth – and he ate the lot. And a second helping too!

A second trick!

The twins' father Isaac was by this time very, very old. He had lost his sight. Before he died, Isaac wanted to give Esau his special blessing, as Isaac's oldest son. But Rebekah wanted Jacob to get this blessing, instead of Esau. As you remember, Jacob was her best-loved son.

So one day, when Esau was away hunting, Rebekah craftily tied bits of hairy animal skin on to Jacob's arms.

Then Jacob went in to see his father, Isaac. Making his voice sound like Esau's, Jacob said, "Father, give me your special blessing now."

But Isaac wanted to make sure it really *was* Esau. "Stretch out your arms," he told Jacob. "Then I can feel your skin. If it's hairy I'll know you really *are* Esau, my oldest son."

Jacob held out his arms, with the animal skins tied to them. When Isaac touched his son's arms, they felt hairy, so he thought it must surely be Esau. So Isaac gave Jacob his special blessing!

Later Esau came in from hunting. When he discovered what Jacob had done, he was furious.

"Jacob has stolen my blessing!" he shouted. "Where is he! I'm going to teach him a lesson he'll never forget!"

Jacob was frightened for his life. He knew he had to get as far as he could from his brother. So Jacob ran away to his uncle, who lived in a distant country.

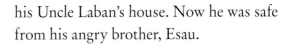

A wonderful dream

One night, while he was on the run, Jacob lay down to sleep, alone in the desert. He found a big rock to use as a pillow. It was all he had. Lying there in the desert, Jacob had a wonderful dream.

In his dream, Jacob saw a stairway to heaven. Angels were walking up and down the stairs. Then God made a promise to Jacob: "I will always look after your family."

As soon as Jacob woke up next morning, he said, "God is surely in this place!"

Then he set off again.

At last, many weeks later, Jacob reached his Uncle Laban's house. Now he was safe from his angry brother, Esau.

Jacob in love

Jacob's Uncle Laban had two daughters, Leah and Rachel. Before he'd been many days in Laban's house, Jacob fell in love with Rachel. He thought she was the most beautiful woman he'd ever met. He wanted to marry her. But Laban told Jacob, "You must work for me seven years – only then will I let you marry my daughter."

So Jacob stayed in Laban's house for seven long years. He worked hard every day, so he could marry Rachel, the beautiful woman he loved.

Jacob has a shock

Finally the time for Jacob's wedding came around. Jacob had worked for Laban for seven whole years.

Jacob's bride wore a thick veil that hid her face. But Jacob had a terrible shock. When his bride took off her veil, he discovered he'd married Leah – not his beloved Rachel.

Laban had tricked Jacob. He'd given him his older daughter, Leah, as his wife – not his younger daughter, Rachel.

Jacob was furious. "What have you done to me?" he shouted at his Uncle Laban.

But Laban said, "Work for me seven years more – *then* I'll give you Rachel!"

Jacob still loved Rachel. He loved her so much that he worked for Laban for seven more years. Then at last Jacob married his beloved Rachel.

Many years had passed, and Jacob decided it was finally time to go home. He took his family, his servants, his flocks and herds, and started out on the long journey back to his father's land.

When Jacob was nearly there, a servant told him, "Your brother Esau is coming to meet you!"

Jacob felt scared. Was Esau still angry with him? "God save me from my brother!" he prayed.

Friends at last!

Next morning Esau arrived at Jacob's camp. Jacob knelt down before his older brother.

But – wonder of wonders – Esau ran to Jacob, and hugged and kissed him. He was delighted to see his brother Jacob again after all these years.

"But tell me, Jacob," said Esau, "who are all these people journeying with you?"

"They are my family," Jacob answered. "My wives – Leah and Rachel – my children, my servants, and my flocks and herds. God has given me many good things."

After this, the quarrelsome brothers lived peacefully as friends!
Genesis 25:19–34, chapters 27–29, 32–33

Joseph and His Brothers

BY THE TIME HE RETURNED from his Uncle Laban's house, Jacob had a big family. Altogether he had twelve sons, and he loved every one of them. But Jacob loved his young son Joseph more than all the rest.

One day Jacob gave Joseph a fantastic coat. How smart he felt! But it made his brothers very jealous. Why did Joseph always get the best presents?

A strange dream

Sometimes Joseph had strange dreams. He loved to tell his brothers these dreams.

One morning he said, "I've had a very odd dream. We were all in the fields at harvest time."

Joseph's brothers gathered round to listen to the tale.

"All of us had bundles of grain," Joseph continued. "But your bundles of grain bowed down to my bundle."

Joseph's brothers grew very angry.

"So you think we should all bow down to you?" asked one brother, furiously.

"You're not king over us!" said another.

The brothers' plot

Some time later Joseph's father called him.

"Your brothers have taken the sheep to new pastures a day's journey away," he said. "Go and take some food for them."

So off went Joseph with a big bag of food for his brothers. While he was still quite a way off, Joseph's brothers saw him coming. How they disliked him!

"Here comes our brother, the dreamer!" said one, mockingly.

"Let's get rid of him," said another.

"Yes – this is our chance!" agreed a third brother.

But one brother wasn't so cruel. "We shouldn't harm Joseph," he said. "Let's just throw him down this dry well."

This brother planned to rescue Joseph later, when the cruel brothers had left.

So when Joseph arrived, his brothers caught hold of him, ripped off his fantastic coat, and threw him down the well.

Sold as a slave

Just then, the brothers saw some traders riding past, on their way to Egypt.

"I've got a great idea!" said one of the brothers. "Let's sell Joseph to those traders!"

"Good thinking!" said another.

So these wicked men sold their own brother, Joseph.

The brothers still hadn't finished plotting. Now they went back to their father, Jacob, and showed him Joseph's torn coat.

"Look, father," they said, pretending to be terribly upset. "We found this coat by the roadside. It's Joseph's special coat – the one you gave him."

The old man nodded sadly.

"A wild animal must have killed Joseph," said one of the brothers, lying to his father.

No one could comfort Jacob, who believed his best-loved son was dead.

Meanwhile the traders took young Joseph to the far-off land of Egypt. Joseph thought he would never see his home again, never see the people he loved.

A trusted servant

When they arrived in Egypt, the traders took Joseph to the marketplace, where people came to buy slaves.

Soon a rich Egyptian called Potiphar saw Joseph, and bought him. He wanted Joseph to work for him in his house.

Joseph was honest and clever. He worked hard for Potiphar, and did everything Potiphar told him.

Potiphar soon found he could trust Joseph. After a time, he put Joseph in charge of his house. Now Joseph told the other servants what to do, and even looked after Potiphar's money.

Joseph was happy for a time. But soon came more trouble. Potiphar's wife started to dislike Joseph, so she lied about him to her husband.

When he heard his wife's tales about Joseph, Potiphar was furious. Without listening to Joseph's side of the story, Potiphar had him thrown into a dark, smelly prison.

Prison!

That might have been the end of Joseph. But in prison, just as in Potiphar's house, people soon trusted and loved him. Before long, the

"The meaning of your dream is this," he told the king's cup-bearer. "In three days, Pharaoh, king of Egypt, will send for you. You will stand by him once more, and give him wine to drink."

Then Joseph spoke sadly to the baker. "I'm very sorry," he told the baker, "but your dream means that in three days Pharaoh, king of Egypt, will send for you – and you will be put to death."

And everything happened just as Joseph had foretold.

"Goodbye," said Joseph to the king's cup-bearer as he left prison. "Please remember me when you stand beside Pharaoh – and speak well of me. I don't want to stay in this horrible prison for the rest of my life."

But the cup-bearer forgot all about Joseph once he was standing beside Pharaoh.

More strange dreams

Then one night Pharaoh, king of Egypt, had two strange dreams. They were so odd that they disturbed him.

"I believe there might be a warning in my dreams," said Pharaoh. "But I've no idea what it is!"

So Pharaoh told his dreams to his wise men.

"This was my first dream," said Pharaoh. "I was standing beside a river, when I saw seven fat cows come out of the water. Then came seven skinny cows – and they gobbled up the seven fat ones."

prison governor even put Joseph in charge of his prison.

One day the governor called Joseph. "I need to tell you about two new prisoners," he said. "One is the king's cup-bearer, and the other the king's baker."

Joseph soon made friends with both of them.

One night these two men each had a strange dream. Their dreams seemed so real to them that the two men were worried. What did their dreams mean?

The two prisoners told their dreams to Joseph. As we know, Joseph had strange dreams when he was a boy; so he listened carefully. Then he explained to the two men what their dreams meant.

"And what was your second dream, O Pharaoh, King of Egypt?" asked the wise men.

"In my other dream, I saw seven good ears of grain growing," said Pharaoh. "Then I saw seven bad ears. As I watched, the bad ears gobbled up the good ears of grain."

Pharaoh turned to his wise men.

"Now tell me the meaning of these strange dreams," he ordered.

"We don't know," said the wise men – at which Pharaoh sent them all away.

At that moment the king's cup-bearer remembered Joseph in prison.

"O Pharaoh, King of Egypt!" he said. "In your prison is a young man who can explain the meaning of dreams. While I was there, he told me what my dream meant."

"Send for him immediately," ordered Pharaoh.

Soon Joseph was standing before Pharaoh. (They cleaned him up and gave him smart new clothes before he was allowed into the palace.)

The dream-teller

"I'm going to describe my dreams to you," said Pharaoh. "Then you must tell me what they mean."

"*I* can't tell you," said Joseph.

Pharaoh scowled furiously.

But Joseph continued, "It is my God who tells me the meaning of dreams."

So Pharaoh retold his dreams, and Joseph listened carefully. He heard about the seven fat cows and the seven lean ones that gobbled them up. He heard about the seven good ears of corn and the seven bad ones that gobbled them up.

When Pharaoh had finished, Joseph spoke.

"O Pharaoh!" said Joseph. "Your two dreams mean precisely the same thing. The seven fat cows are seven years with plentiful harvests. The seven skinny cows are seven poor years, when there will be no harvest. The seven good ears of corn are also seven years of plenty, and the seven poor ears of corn are seven hungry years."

Pharaoh listened in silence.

"God has sent these dreams to warn you," Joseph explained. "For seven years of plenty, everyone will have all they need to eat. But the seven years of hunger, when there will be no harvest, will be terrible. There will be nothing to eat."

Pharaoh looked worried.

"You've told me what my dreams mean, Joseph," said Pharaoh. "Now please tell me what I can do to keep my people from starving during the bad years."

"You will have to find a wise and clever person," said Joseph. "This wise person will govern the land of Egypt for you. He must make sure your officers set aside part of the grain harvested in each of the seven good years."

"Where will we put all this grain?" asked Pharaoh.

"You must build great storehouses for the grain," Joseph told him. "Save up the grain until the seven bad years come. Then open up the storehouses and sell the good grain to your hungry people, so they can make bread to eat."

Joseph the wise

Then Pharaoh did something amazing. He took off his royal ring and put it on Joseph's finger. He had decided Joseph was the wise and clever person he needed. So Pharaoh made Joseph his chief minister!

For the next seven years, Joseph set aside part of the grain harvest every year and put it in great storehouses.

When the seven years of hunger came, the storehouses were opened up, and people could buy grain. The people of Egypt had enough food, even during the worst years of famine.

When the hungry years came, Jacob and his family – who were still living in Canaan – couldn't get enough grain. Then Jacob heard there was plenty of food in Egypt

"Go to Egypt and buy grain," Jacob told his sons. So the ten brothers set off for Egypt to try to find food. Their youngest brother, Benjamin, stayed at home with his aged father.

When Joseph's brothers arrived in Egypt looking for grain, he knew straight away who thcy were. But they didn't recognize him – it was such a long time since they'd seen him.

"You're all spies," he said, to test them.

"No!" they said. "We've come from our home simply to buy food."

They explained to Joseph about Jacob and the rest of their family in Canaan. Joseph gave them some food.

But he said, "If you come back to Egypt for more grain, you must bring your youngest brother, too."

The brothers took the grain to Jacob in Canaan. But the time came when Jacob's family needed more food.

The brothers returned to Egypt, this time bringing young Benjamin with them. When they arrived, Joseph ordered his servants to prepare a feast for them.

Joseph's trick

Joseph came to the feast and saw Benjamin for the first time in many years. He was so happy to see his youngest brother again!

Joseph gave his brothers all the grain they wanted. And still they didn't recognize him!

This time Joseph played a trick on them. He hid a silver cup inside Benjamin's sack of grain.

Then Joseph shouted, "My silver cup is

missing! Someone's stolen it."

Joseph ordered his servants to search the brothers' sacks of grain. Of course, Joseph's servants soon discovered the missing cup in Benjamin's sack.

Joseph said sternly, "Benjamin cannot go home with the rest of you."

But Benjamin's brothers begged Joseph, "Please don't keep him in Egypt. It will kill our old father, Jacob."

Joseph saw that his brothers had changed. They were no longer unkind, as they had been when they had sold him to traders years before.

"I am your brother Joseph!" he told them finally. "You sold me as a slave, but God sent me here to Egypt to help the people. Now hurry home and bring our father here."

How surprised Jacob was to hear the brothers' story. And how glad he was to see his beloved son Joseph again, when he journeyed to Egypt!

This is how God's people, the Israelites, came to live in the land of Egypt.

Genesis chapters 37, 39–45

The Baby in the Basket

WE HAVE READ how Jacob's family came to Egypt during the time of Joseph the dreamer. Because of the terrible hunger, they left Canaan and journeyed to live in this strange land.

Pharaoh, king of Egypt, had made Joseph his chief minister. He welcomed the family of Joseph – the children of Israel, the "Israelites".

But after the Israelites had been living in Egypt for many years, a new pharaoh, who did not like them, came to the throne.

"There are just too many of these Israelites," he said. "They are getting far too strong. We must make them work hard for us, so they become no stronger."

So Pharaoh forced the Israelites to make bricks for him, and to build him great cities.

The Israelites had to make bricks out of clay from the river banks, and use chopped straw to hold the clay together. They baked the bricks hard under the hot sun.

Egyptian soldiers beat the Israelites, to make them work faster.

But this wasn't enough for Pharaoh. He saw the Israelites were still growing in number.

So Pharaoh gave a terrible order.

"Take every Israelite baby boy and throw him into the River Nile," he said. "Then no more Israelite men will grow up in my kingdom of Egypt."

A basket for a baby

An Israelite mother called Jochebed had a beautiful baby boy. She was afraid Egyptian soldiers would come and snatch her baby away. How could she save him?

At first Jochebed hid her little boy in the house. But as he grew, Jochebed was afraid a passing Egyptian soldier might hear the baby crying and take him away.

So Jochebed dreamed up a plan.

"We'll make a little basket from rushes," she explained to her daughter, Miriam. "Then we'll float the basket among the reeds in the river, just where the princess of Egypt comes to bathe every morning."

So Miriam and her mother set to work, making a strong basket.

"Let's coat it with slime and tar," said Jochebed. "Then water won't seep through the gaps and sink the basket."

At last the special basket was finished.

"Now let's put baby in," said Jochebed.

She lifted her tiny boy and laid him gently in the basket. While he was still fast asleep, they hurried down to the river.

Jochebed waited till nobody was around to see what they were doing.

"Here are some reeds," said Miriam. "Let's put baby amongst them. Then he'll be well hidden."

They placed the basket on the water; it floated gently.

Jochebed turned to go.

"Miriam," she said, "hide nearby and watch to see what happens to our baby."

So Miriam hid in the bulrushes. She saw the little basket bobbing in the river. Her baby brother slept peacefully.

A royal discovery

Suddenly Miriam heard voices. She peeped out and saw the princess of Egypt coming with her maids to bathe in the river.

All at once, the princess glimpsed something in the reeds.

"What's that?" she asked. "It looks like a little boat made of rushes."

"Shall I go and find out, Your Majesty?" asked a maid.

"Yes – please fetch it here for me," said the princess.

The maid ran to the water's edge. She lifted the basket carefully out of the water.

It was surprisingly heavy! She carried the basket to her mistress.

The princess saw the sleeping boy inside. He woke up and started to cry.

"What a beautiful baby!" said the princess. "Let me hold him."

The princess lifted the baby out and cradled him gently in her arms.

"Hush," she whispered, "don't cry! Please don't cry!"

Then she said to her maid, "This must be one of those Israelite boys who were supposed to be thrown in the river. How I wish he were mine. He's so, so sweet!"

Miriam had been watching all this time from her hiding place. Now she crept out and stood shyly in front of the princess.

"O Princess, would you like a nurse for the baby?" Miriam asked politely. "I know someone who would look after him so well."

The princess looked again at the baby – and in that moment decided to keep him.

"Go!" she said to Miriam. "Bring me someone to help care for the baby."

Miriam ran straight home. Her mother looked up startled when she burst in.

"Whatever's the matter?" she asked.

"Great news, Mother!" said Miriam, happily. "The princess came down to bathe and found our baby."

"Is he safe?" asked Jochebed anxiously.

"Oh yes!" said Miriam. "The princess even wants a nurse to look after him. You have to come back with me."

Jochebed hurried back to the river with her daughter Miriam. There she saw the princess, with the little baby still cradled in her arms.

"Your Majesty," she said, "my daughter says you're looking for a nurse for the child."

A nurse for the baby

The princess smiled.

"Yes, she's quite right. I came upon this poor baby floating in a basket. Now I need to find him a good nurse.

"When the little boy is older," the princess continued, "I will bring him up as my own son. Could you look after him for me until he's grown into a young man?"

Jochebed was so happy! She held out her arms for the baby. The princess gave him to Jochebed – and the baby smiled. It was his mother!

"Look after him well," the princess said to Jochebed. "I will pay you. Then, when the time comes, bring him to the palace to live with me."

Jochebed and Miriam went off happily. Now the baby boy could grow up at home with them safely.

So the boy lived peacefully with his own family, growing stronger as each month passed. But the princess of Egypt never forgot him. She planned for the time when he would come to live with her in the royal palace.

Prince of Egypt

Finally the day arrived when Jochebed took her son to the princess. Sadly, she said goodbye.

"I will call you 'Moses'," said the princess proudly. "It means 'taken from the water'!"

After this, Moses was brought up as a prince in the palace of the king of Egypt. He wore fine clothes and ate splendid food. He learned many new things, and grew up strong and wise.

But Moses never forgot he was the son of an Israelite slave. He felt so sorry for his people when he saw them working hard, making bricks in the hot sun.

"One day," thought Moses, "I will rescue my people. I will be their leader."
Exodus 2:1–10

Moses Sees a Burning Bush

SO MOSES GREW UP as a prince in the court of Pharaoh, king of Egypt. The princess of Egypt had adopted him as her son, and brought him up as a prince of Egypt. But Moses never forgot that he was the son of an Israelite.

One day, when he was still a young man, Moses was walking near the mud pits where Israelites had to make bricks for Pharaoh. As he passed, he noticed an Egyptian cruelly beating an Israelite workman. Moses was so angry that he struck the Egyptian dead.

Moses was very frightened. He had to escape the city before Egyptian soldiers could catch him. He went as far as he could from Egypt to find safety.

Now Moses married and started to work as a shepherd. He took his flock of sheep out into the lonely desert. Day after day he looked after them. He led his sheep to water; he scared away any wild animals; and he protected his flock at night.

While the sheep were searching for grass to eat, Moses remembered fondly his home in Egypt. Working as a shepherd was so different from his life as a prince in the court of Pharaoh, king of Egypt.

Back in Egypt, Pharaoh was making life even harder for the Israelites. They prayed to God to help them. The Israelites longed to escape from Egypt, to become free to worship God. And God heard their prayers.

Holy ground

One day, as Moses was leading his flock through the lonely desert, he came to a great mountain called Sinai.

He noticed a bush nearby was on fire. But there was something strange about it! He watched carefully – then Moses realized what was so odd. The bush was on fire – but it didn't burn away. It burned and burned – but never burned up.

"How extraordinary!" Moses thought. "Why doesn't the bush burn away?"

Suddenly he heard a voice calling, "Moses! Moses!"

"Here I am!" Moses answered.

"Come no nearer!" ordered the voice, sternly. "Take off your sandals. The place where you're standing is holy… I am the God of Abraham, the God of Isaac, and of Jacob."

Moses was trembling now. He listened very carefully.

"I have seen how cruelly the Egyptians are treating my people, the Israelites," God told him. "Now I'm going to help them. I want you to go to Pharaoh, king of Egypt, and tell him to let my people go free. Then you, Moses, will lead my people out of Egypt – and bring them to this mountain. To Mount Sinai."

But Moses wasn't prepared to do this. He was scared!

He would have to return to Egypt, where he had killed a man. And stand before the mighty king of Egypt.

Moses argues with God

"Who, me?" answered Moses. "I couldn't possibly do that! *Never!*"

"But Moses, I will help you," said God.

"What am I supposed to say when the Israelites ask, 'Who sent you? What is his name?'" asked Moses. "What shall I tell them?"

"I am God Almighty. Tell them I have sent you," God answered. "I was with Abraham and Sarah. I was with Abraham's son, Isaac. I was with Isaac's son, Jacob. Now I will be with my people, Israel."

Moses thought about this.

"But God, I'm no good at speaking in public," he said. "I never know what to say… I get nervous. I stutter and stammer."

"Moses, who helps people to speak?" God asked. "When you speak, Moses, I will give you the words to say."

But Moses went on arguing.

"Lord, please send someone else – not me!" he pleaded.

By now God was getting quite cross!

"Then how about your brother Aaron? He's a good speaker. He can speak for you," said God. "You can tell Aaron what to say – then let him do the talking for you."

At last Moses agreed to do what God wanted. He left his sheep. He left the desert. He took his family back to Egypt.

Moses went to Pharaoh's palace, taking his brother Aaron with him.

Exodus chapters 3–4

God Frees the Israelites

AFTER GOD SPOKE TO HIM at the burning bush in the desert, Moses returned to Egypt. He marched up to Pharaoh's palace, with his brother Aaron. They stood together boldly before Pharaoh, king of Egypt.

God gave Moses the words to say, and Moses repeated them to Aaron.

"Let my people go!"

"O mighty Pharaoh!" said Aaron. "It is wrong to keep people as slaves." He paused.

Then he spoke loud and clear. "Here is what the God of Israel says: 'Let my people go so they can worship me in the desert!'"

"But I don't even know this God of yours," replied Pharaoh angrily. "He can't tell *me* what to do. I'm certainly not letting my Israelite workers go free!"

Pharaoh was furious that these two Israelites – Moses and Aaron – had come to his palace cheekily telling him what to do.

So he called in his captains: "Force my Israelite workers to toil harder," he said. "If they have enough time to worship their God, then they're wasting *my* time. Make them work harder than ever."

Pharaoh's captains obeyed the king; they made life even harder for the Israelites.

Moses was fed up and disappointed. He had expected Pharaoh to listen to God's instructions – and let his people go.

"Pharaoh has just made our people work even harder," Moses complained to God.

"Then go back to Pharaoh," God told Moses. "If he doesn't let my people go, his people – the Egyptians – will be made to suffer terrible things."

A gobbling snake

So Moses and Aaron returned to Pharaoh's palace.

"Throw down your stick," God instructed Aaron.

Aaron did so – and the stick immediately turned into a snake.

Pharaoh's magicians copied him and threw down their sticks. They turned into snakes too!

But then Aaron's snake gobbled up all the rest of the snakes!

Still Pharaoh didn't do as God told him.

Then God sent some very hard times on Egypt.

Moses and Aaron went to Pharaoh's palace yet again. Once more they stood before Pharaoh, king of Egypt.

"O mighty Pharaoh, the God of Israel says: 'Let my people go!'" said Aaron.

"Do you think I'm going to do what your God says?" Pharaoh answered. "Forget it! I need the Israelites to make my bricks and build my palaces. Now get out of my palace and stop bothering me."

"If you disobey," Moses warned Pharaoh, "God will turn the water of the River Nile into blood."

"I will *not* let your people go," repeated Pharaoh.

So God turned the water of the Nile to blood. No one could drink the water.

Moses and Aaron went to the palace again. Once more they stood before Pharaoh, king of Egypt.

"Ask your God to turn the blood back to water," Pharaoh said to Moses. "When he does, I will let your people go."

So Moses prayed, "Lord God, please turn the blood back to river water."

And God did as Moses asked.

But *still* Pharaoh did not let the Israelites go free.

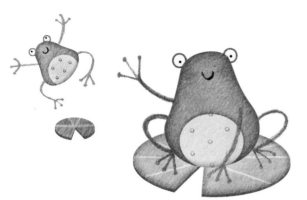

Frogs

So Moses and Aaron went to the palace again. Once more they stood before Pharaoh, king of Egypt.

"Let my people go!" said Aaron. "If you don't, God will send frogs all over your land."

"I will not let your people go!" said Pharaoh.

So God sent frogs into his palace – and all over his land.

Pharaoh called for Moses.

"Get your God to take away the frogs," said Pharaoh. "*Then* I will let your people go."

So Moses prayed to God, "Lord God, please take away all these frogs."

And the frogs went.

Still Pharaoh didn't let the Israelites go.

Flies

Moses and Aaron went to the palace again. Once more they stood before Pharaoh, king of Egypt.

"Let my people go," said Moses. "If you disobey, God will send countless swarms of flies all across your land."

"I will not let your people go," said Pharaoh.

So God sent swarms of flies into Pharaoh's palace – and all over the land of Egypt.

Then Pharaoh called for Moses. "Ask your God to take away the flies," he said. "*Then* I will let your people go."

Moses prayed, "Lord God, take away every one of these flies!"

The flies vanished.

But *still* Pharaoh did not let the Israelite people go.

So Moses and Aaron went to the palace yet again. Once more they stood before Pharaoh, king of Egypt.

"Let my people go!" said Moses. "If you don't, God will make every living creature in your land fall ill."

"I will not let your people go," repeated Pharaoh.

So every animal in Egypt fell ill.

Pharaoh called again for Moses.

"Ask your God to make the animals well again," he said. "*Then* I *really will* let your people go."

So Moses asked God to make the animals well again. He did so. The disease left them.

51

But still Pharaoh did not let the Israelites go.

Next painful boils and sores appeared on the Egyptians' skin. Huge hailstones fell on the fields, destroying the crops. Grasshoppers called locusts appeared in countless swarms. They ate every leaf on every tree and every stalk of grain, till there was nothing left to eat.

Then darkness came across the land of Egypt. Yet still Pharaoh did not obey God.

Passover

Finally God told Moses, "The firstborn of every living creature in Egypt – human and animal – is going to die. Tell the Israelites to kill a lamb for dinner tonight. They must mark their doorways with the lamb's blood."

That very night, God was going to free the Israelites. They marked their doorways with lamb's blood, and ate a special meal of lamb, as God had instructed Moses.

Afterwards, the Israelites remembered this night every year, at a feast they called "Passover". They remembered that God had saved them.

That night, the eldest son in every Egyptian family died. Even Pharaoh's son died. Only the sons of the Israelites lived.

Now at last Pharaoh knew the God of the Israelites was more powerful than him.

He called Moses to his palace for the very last time.

"Take your people out of Egypt!" he told Moses. "Hurry! Otherwise we will *all* fall sick and die."

So at last the Israelites left Egypt. They set out on a long journey, to the land that God had promised them, taking with them their sheep and cattle.

Moses led his people out of Egypt.
Exodus chapters 5–12

Moses Leads His People Out of Egypt

IT WAS THE MIDDLE of the night.

Every Israelite family hurriedly packed up everything they owned. Then they left Egypt, with Moses leading the way. They went very quietly, so the Egyptians wouldn't hear them creeping away.

The Israelites walked day and night to escape from Pharaoh. But when the Egyptians realized the Israelites had disappeared, they grew angry. Now there was nobody to work for them, making bricks and building palaces.

Pharaoh, king of Egypt, changed his mind again. He ordered his army and his chariots to chase after the Israelites and drag them back to Egypt.

Soon the Israelites reached the shores of the great Red Sea. There they stopped. Now they had a new problem: how could they ever cross the deep water of the Red Sea that spread out in front of them?

Suddenly, the Israelites saw clouds of dust behind them. They heard horses' hooves.

It was Pharaoh and his army! The Egyptians were speeding up in their chariots. They were coming to force the Israelites back to Egypt to work for them once again.

The Red Sea

The Israelites were terrified.

"What do we do now?" they demanded of Moses. "We can't escape! The Red Sea is in front of us – and Pharaoh and his mighty army behind us. We will all die here, for sure!"

"Don't be scared!" said Moses. "God will help us again."

And God gave Moses special instructions.

"Stretch out your hand!" he told Moses. Moses stretched out his hand.

At once, a mighty wind blew a dry path through the Red Sea and the waters divided. Now there was a clear roadway leading across the sea. The Israelites started to walk safely across the seabed on dry land.

Soon they had all reached the other side.

But Pharaoh and his soldiers were still chasing the Israelites. They started along the pathway across the Red Sea.

When every Israelite was safely across, Moses lowered his hand. The wind dropped and the water flowed back onto the seabed.

Pharaoh, his chariots, and all his soldiers drowned in the sea. They were never seen again.

At last the Israelites were safe from Pharaoh and the Egyptians. They danced for joy. They sang, "Our God is always with us. He saved us!"

Bitter water

But the Israelites still had a very long way to go. They trudged on through the hot desert.

Everyone was thirsty; their tongues felt dry.

For three days the Israelites searched for water, until at last they found a well. They drew some water. *Yeeuchh!* It was so bitter they couldn't drink it.

Some Israelites went off to find Moses.

"What are we going to do now?" they demanded. "Do you want us all to die of thirst here in the desert? We were better off in Egypt. At least we had water to drink!"

God showed Moses a bit of wood lying on the ground. Moses threw it into the well.

Someone drew another bucket of water from the well and tasted it. It was no longer bitter!

Now everyone could drink as much good water as they wanted.

Food from heaven

Next the Israelites ran out of bread. They had nothing left to eat. Some felt faint with hunger.

People came angrily to Moses again. "Why did you lead us into this awful desert?" they demanded. "We're all going to starve to death here – that's for certain! We should have stayed in Egypt! At least we got enough to eat there!"

"You won't die," Moses told them. "God will take care of you. Just wait till morning – then you'll see something *quite* wonderful!"

Sure enough, when they woke in the morning, they discovered the earth was covered with white, powdery stuff.

One man put some on his finger and licked it. It tasted sweet – and good! Soon they were all eating it. The Israelites called this food "manna".

After this, they found manna on the ground every morning. God provided this special food for his people for as long as they were in the desert.

Exodus 12:1–42, 13:17–22, 14:1–31, 16:1–35

Rules to Live By

THE ISRAELITES TRUDGED on through the hot desert for week after week. At last they reached Mount Sinai. The mountain was so high that the top was often hidden in clouds.

This was the very place where Moses had discovered the burning bush, many years before. Here, at Mount Sinai, the Israelites set up camp and rested.

Moses climbs the mountain

Moses decided to climb the mountain on his own, to meet God.

When Moses reached the top, God spoke to him solemnly.

"I led your people out of Egypt," God told him. "I looked after your people in the desert. I gave them water to drink and manna to eat."

Then God made a wonderful promise to Moses and the people of Israel: "I will be your God and you shall be my people. You must live in a way that pleases me."

Then God said, "I am going to give you my rules for living. You must write down these rules on big, flat stones."

So Moses wrote out God's special rules for living on these stones.

We call the rules the "Ten Commandments":

1. *I am the Lord, your God; I freed you from Egypt. Do not worship any God except me.*
2. *Do not make idols. Do not bow down and worship idols.*
3. *Do not misuse my name.*
4. *Keep one day of rest each week. You have six days when you can work; but the seventh belongs to me, your God.*
5. *Respect your father and your mother.*
6. *Do not kill.*
7. *Be faithful to your husband or wife.*
8. *Do not steal.*
9. *Do not tell lies about other people.*
10. *Do not wish to have anything that belongs to another person.*

Moses wrote all this down.

A golden calf

Moses was away so long on top of Mount Sinai that the Israelites thought he was never coming back.

Some people said to Aaron, "Make a golden calf for us to worship!"

So Aaron told everyone to bring him their gold rings, gold bracelets, and earrings. He melted them all down and made a golden calf. Aaron set up this statue in the middle of the Israelite camp.

People started to bow down to the golden calf, sing to it, and dance around it. They forgot all about the God who had brought them out of Egypt; instead they began to worship the calf Aaron had made out of gold rings and bracelets!

At last Moses came down from Mount Sinai.

As he clambered down the mountain, he thought he heard singing and shouting. He couldn't understand what all the noise was.

Then, when he climbed a bit further down, he caught sight of the golden calf.

Moses was so angry that he threw to the ground the two stones with God's rules on them.

They smashed into tiny pieces.

When the Israelites realized how much they had angered God, they told him they were sorry.

Now Moses had to climb Mount Sinai a second time to get a fresh set of stones with God's rules written on them.

A special tent

Back up on Mount Sinai God had given Moses another important message.

"You must build a huge tent," God told him, "where my people can pray."

While Moses and the Israelites had been in the desert, they had no special building where they could pray.

God described to Moses exactly how the tent was to be built, and what should go inside it.

Lots of different materials were used to make the tent. The Israelites gladly gave Moses wood, cloth, silver, and gold they had brought with them from Egypt to help build it. They called it the "tabernacle".

It was built so it was easy for the Israelites to take it apart and put it back together again. When they moved on, they packed up the tent and took it with them.

They also made a special wooden box, covered in gold, to keep the Ten Commandments in. This box had gold angels on top, and was called the "ark of the covenant".

They kept the ark of the covenant in a curtained-off room inside the great tent. No one was allowed in there except the chief priest, just once a year.

Aaron became the first chief priest. He wore special clothes to show he was a priest.

"Now journey on to the country I have promised you," God told the Israelites. "Remember – I will always be with you."

The journey continues

So the Israelites packed their tents, left Mount Sinai, and moved on. The journey was long and dangerous, and they had many more adventures.

The Israelites wandered through the desert for forty years. They often grumbled and complained.

Sometimes they disobeyed God. But God never gave up on them.

After all the long years of wandering, Moses finally brought the Israelites to a high mountain, called Mount Nebo. From its top, they could see into the land God had promised them.

But Moses died on Mount Nebo, before he could enter the Promised Land.

Exodus chapters 19–20, 26, 32, 34

Joshua Captures a Great City

AT LAST THE ISRAELITES reached the River Jordan. On the opposite side of the river lay the country God had promised them – the land of Canaan.

The Israelites had been wandering in the desert for forty years since escaping from Egypt. Now they finally reached the Promised Land. How happy they were! They gave thanks to God.

The time had come for the Israelites to enter their new land. But now they had a new problem: how to cross the River Jordan. There were no bridges and no boats – and the water was running fast and high.

Crossing the river

God gave the priests special instructions: "Walk into the waters of the Jordan, carrying on your shoulders the ark of the covenant – the precious box containing the Ten Commandments."

The priests did just as God told them – and at once God cleared a dry path through the water. The people of Israel – men, women, and children, with all their flocks and herds, and all their belongings – followed the priests across. They walked on dry ground to the opposite bank of the river. Once they were all safely over, the waters of the river flooded back again.

The Israelites had finally arrived in the Promised Land!

The very first place the Israelites came to in Canaan was the great old city of Jericho. It had high, thick walls and mighty gates, and watchful guards were posted everywhere. The gates were all shut tight against the Israelites. No one could enter or leave the city.

The Israelites decided to set up camp outside the huge walls of Jericho. There they celebrated the festival of Passover, remembering how God had set them free from slavery in Egypt years before, in the time of Moses.

Joshua was the new leader of the Israelites. God explained to him how to capture the city of Jericho.

"Each day, for six days, you must march your people around the city walls," God told Joshua. "Seven priests will march at the front. Next will come the men carrying the ark of the covenant. The priests must take with them their trumpets made from

rams' horns, and blow them as you march. Everyone else will keep quiet.

"On the seventh day, everyone will march right around the city seven times. The priests will then blow one long, loud blast on their trumpets – and everybody else must shout at the top of their voices. If you do all this," God promised, "the walls of Jericho will fall – and the whole city will be yours."

So each day the Israelites marched around the walls of Jericho, just as God had said. Each night they returned to their camp.

The people of Jericho watched. They were *so* puzzled! What ever were the Israelites up to now?

A great shout

On the seventh day, the Israelites marched around the towering walls of Jericho seven times, following the priests and the ark of the covenant. Round and round they marched. Then, the seventh and last time, the priests blasted on their trumpets, and every Israelite shouted at the top of his or her voice. What a row!

That moment, down crashed the walls – just as God had promised. And it wasn't long before the Israelite soldiers had captured the whole city of Jericho.

This was just the first of Joshua's many victories in Canaan, the Promised Land.

With Joshua leading them, the Israelites gradually took over the entire land. Now it was their country.

Joshua chapters 3–4, 5:13 – 6:27

Samson the Strong

AFTER JOSHUA DIED, the Israelites began to forget about God and everything he had done for them. So God allowed the fierce Philistines to attack their country.

One day, God sent an angel to speak to an Israelite named Manoah.

"Your wife is going to have a baby son," the angel told Manoah. "He will be very special. When he grows up, he will protect your people, the Israelites, from your enemies, the Philistines."

When the boy was born, his parents named him Samson. They never, ever cut his hair. Manoah and his wife allowed Samson's hair to grow very, very long, to show that he was someone who had special work to do for God.

A donkey's jawbone

Samson grew up to be particularly strong. One day, he killed a lion using just his bare hands. Samson knew God had made him specially strong so that he could fight the Philistines. And over the years, that's exactly what he did.

Once, Samson saw the Philistines' fields of grain standing ripe to harvest. So he set light to some foxes' tails, and then let them run free all over the fields. Soon the Philistines' crops were ablaze: that year there was no harvest!

Another time, Samson faced one thousand Philistine soldiers. He picked up a donkey's jawbone, and started to hit the Philistines with it. He soon beat the whole bunch of them! Samson always got the better of his enemies.

Whenever the Philistines tried to catch Samson, or trap him, he always managed to

escape. He was simply too strong for them!

The Philistines became desperate to capture Samson. How could they ever entrap this super-strong man?

At last the Philistines got a chance. One day, Samson fell in love with a beautiful Philistine girl, named Delilah. He had eyes for her only; he wouldn't be parted from her.

When they heard Samson was in love with Delilah, five Philistine kings went to her.

"We'll give you hundreds of silver coins," the kings told Delilah. "All you have to do is to persuade Samson to tell you exactly what makes him so strong."

Delilah agreed at once. She'd never dreamt of having so much money!

Next time she met Samson, Delilah asked slyly, "What makes you so very strong, Samson dearest?"

But he joked with her. Samson wouldn't tell Delilah the *real* reason he was so strong.

Each time Delilah asked him to explain the secret of his strength, Samson made up a different story.

"If you tie me up with new bowstrings," he said one time, "I'll be just as weak as anyone else."

She tried this – but Samson snapped the strings as if they were thin strands of wool.

Another time he told Delilah, "Tie me up with a brand new rope – *then* I'll lose all my strength."

She tried this too – but Samson broke the rope as if it were a bit of cotton.

The third time she asked, Samson told her, "Weave my hair into a loom – then I'll be no stronger than a newborn baby."

Delilah tried this too – but Samson yanked his hair out of the loom with no trouble at all!

Delilah tried every way she could think of to discover Samson's secret – but he stayed as strong as ever.

Samson is shaved

"If you won't tell me what makes you so strong," Delilah complained, "it shows you don't *really* love me at all."

She begged and sulked and whined, until finally foolish Samson gave in.

"If someone *completely* shaved my head," he whispered in Delilah's ear, "I'd lose all my strength. I'm strong because of my long, uncut hair."

That very night, as soon as Samson was snoring in his sleep, Delilah called in a barber to cut off his hair.

Snip, snip, snip! Soon Samson's beautiful, long hair lay all over the floor. And in that very moment, Samson lost all his strength.

The Philistines were waiting outside the door for Delilah's signal. They burst in, tied Samson up, and dragged him off. No trouble at all! He had no strength now.

Samson was soon chained up in prison in Gaza, the Philistines' capital city. They punished him by making him work very hard for them.

Then one night the Philistines threw a great party for their god, Dagon.

"Let's bring Samson here from the prison," someone shouted. "We could have a good laugh at the strong man who's now as weak as a baby!"

So guards brought Samson from jail to the temple where the party was being held. It was crowded with people.

The Philistines laughed and jeered when they saw Samson coming.

"Aren't you supposed to be so strong!" they mocked. "How come you're in chains?"

Samson's last victory

But while he'd been in prison, Samson's hair had begun to grow again. The Philistines had never noticed! Soon his hair was just as long as it had been before.

Samson heard the Philistines taunting him.

"Help me just once more," he prayed. "Lord, give me back my old strength!"

And God did as Samson asked.

Samson pushed with all his might against the pillars that held up the building. The pillars started to tip. The walls fell. The roof collapsed – right on top of the party-goers.

Every Philistine inside the temple was killed. And so was Samson. It was his final great feat of strength.

Judges chapters 13, 16

Samuel Listens to God

ON THE TOP OF A HILL in the Promised Land stood God's Tent, the tabernacle. There lived the priests who taught the Israelite people how to love and obey God. Every year they held a great festival there, and many of the people came to celebrate.

One year a man brought his wife, Hannah, to the festival. She was very sad because she had no children. She longed more than anything else to have a baby boy.

Eli, the chief priest, watched Hannah as she knelt down and talked to God.

"God, give me a little son," Hannah begged. "Let me have a baby boy. When he grows up, I will give him back to you, to help you."

"Go home, Hannah," said old Eli gently. "God has been listening to you."

and day. Samuel learned how to fill them with oil. The priests also taught Samuel to read and write.

Each year, when the great festival came around, Samuel's mother, Hannah would visit. She loved seeing her son again. Every year Hannah brought Samuel a new coat.

A voice in the night

One night, after he had been at the tabernacle a few years, Samuel was asleep in bed.

A voice called him, "Samuel, Samuel!"

Samuel woke with a start. He thought it was Eli calling – and ran in to the old man.

"Here I am, Eli!" he said. "You called me."

"I didn't, Samuel," said Eli. "Go and lie down again."

A boy for Hannah

Hannah went home much happier. Now she felt sure she would have the baby son she so much wanted.

And she did.

"We will call our little boy Samuel," she said when her baby arrived. "I'll give him to God to help in the tabernacle, as I promised."

So when Samuel had grown big enough, Hannah took him back to God's Tent.

Eli the priest was waiting.

"Here is the child I asked God for," Hannah said. "The Lord heard when I prayed. Now I've brought young Samuel to you to help you serve God in his great Tent."

Samuel learnt quickly everything that Eli wanted him to do. He was soon helping the priests with their jobs. The oil lamps were supposed to burn brightly in the tent night

Samuel went back to his bed. But once more he heard a voice call, "Samuel!"

The boy ran to Eli again, saying, "Here I am again, Eli – you really *did* call me."

The old priest said once more, "No, I didn't call you! Go back and lie down again."

Then a third time the voice came, "Samuel, Samuel!"

And a third time Samuel went in to Eli.

"Here am I, Eli! I'm *sure* I heard you call," he said.

By now Eli had had time to think it over. He realized it must be God calling to Samuel.

"Go and lie down, Samuel," said Eli. "If you hear this voice calling again say, 'Speak, Lord – your helper is listening.'"

Samuel felt a bit afraid when Eli said this. But he went back to his room to lie down.

He listened – and soon, in the darkness, the voice came again, "Samuel! Samuel!"

This time the boy answered just as Eli had told him, "Speak, Lord – your helper is listening!"

And then God did speak to Samuel.

There was very sad news. God told Samuel that Eli and his sons had done wrong and he was going to punish them. Samuel felt frightened: he didn't want to tell Eli about this.

But in the morning Eli asked what God had said to him, so Samuel had to tell him. The old man was sad.

"Things will be as God has decided," said old Eli the priest.

1 Samuel chapters 1, 3

Samuel Finds a King

WHEN SAMUEL GREW UP, he became the ruler of his people, the Israelites. He taught them how to live in a way that pleased God.

One day, some people went to Samuel. "You're very old now," they told him. "Your sons are not good men; we don't want them to rule us. Now we'd like to have a king to reign over us."

"If you have a king, you'll soon start complaining about him," Samuel told them. "He'll do just as all kings do – he'll want lots of your money."

"But we want to be like all the other countries," the people said. "We want a king to rule us."

"All right," Samuel said at last, "I'll find you a king. But don't say I haven't warned you what will happen!"

The lost donkeys

At this time there lived a young man called Saul. He was taller than any other man in the land. Saul was the son of a rich man called Kish, who owned many flocks of sheep and herds of cattle, as well as some wild donkeys.

One day Kish sent for Saul. "Some of my donkeys have escaped," he told his son. "Take one of the servants and see if you can find them."

So Saul and his servant set off in search of the missing donkeys.

They journeyed all over the country – but couldn't find the donkeys anywhere.

"We ought to go home now," Saul said to the servant. "If my father thinks we've got lost too, he'll send out a search party for us."

But now they had a new problem: neither of them knew the way home!

Then the servant had an idea.

"We're close to where Samuel lives," he told Saul. "Let's go and ask him the best way home."

"But we've nothing to give him as a thank-you present," said Saul.

"I've got a silver coin," said the servant.

"We could give him that."

So they set out to find Samuel's house.

When he opened the door, Samuel looked up at Saul. He was head and shoulders taller than his servant.

"Now, this young man really looks like a king!" Samuel thought to himself. "People would love to have a man like *this* to rule them."

The big feast

Samuel turned to Saul.

"We're having a great feast," he said. "Please come along. Don't worry about your donkeys – they've already been tracked

down. What's more important is that you're just the man the people of Israel are looking for."

Saul was astonished. "Whatever can he mean?" he thought to himself.

Saul went along to the feast anyway. Then he got another surprise: Samuel put him in the top seat! Everyone looked at Saul – and liked what they saw.

"Saul would be a king who was afraid of nobody," they said to each other. "He'd soon get rid of our enemies."

"The people are demanding a king," Samuel told Saul. "He needs to be young, strong, and fearless. But he must also please God. When the time comes, *you* shall be king. Until then, go home and wait quietly."

So Saul went home and waited, as Samuel told him.

A royal crown

After some time, Samuel called for Saul.

When the Israelites saw Saul again, they still thought he was the man they wanted for king.

"Saul could lead us into battle," they said. "We'd follow him anywhere!"

"Here's the king God has chosen for you!" announced Samuel. "There's no one like him in the whole of Israel."

"God save the king!" people shouted.

So Saul became the first king of the people of Israel. The man who went in search of wild donkeys found a royal crown!

1 Samuel chapters 8–10

The Shepherd Who Beat a Giant

KING SAUL DID NOT rule well.

After a time, God told Samuel, "You will have to find a new king to rule Israel."

Now there was a young shepherd boy named David. He lived with his family in the little town of Bethlehem. David had seven grown-up brothers.

David could sing beautifully and play the harp wonderfully. He was also a good shepherd. He guarded his flocks well. He had a sling, and with it he could hurl a stone a long way. One day a lion and a bear came hunting for David's sheep. He killed both the lion and the bear with his sling.

David was the bravest of the brothers, although he was the youngest.

One day God said to Samuel, "Go to Bethlehem and find a man called Jesse. One of his sons will become the next king of Israel."

So Samuel went to Bethlehem.

Jesse threw a great feast for him. Then he paraded before Samuel his seven grown-up sons, all strong and handsome. But God wanted none of them.

Samuel was puzzled. He turned to Jesse. "Are all your sons here?" asked Samuel.

"All except David, my youngest," said

Jesse. "He's away minding the sheep."

"Fetch him too!" said Samuel.

So one of his brothers went to fetch David.

When the youngest son ran in, Samuel thought, "*This* is the boy God has chosen. When he's old enough, he will be the king of Israel."

The shepherd and the giant

Soon Israel's old enemies, the Philistines, came to do battle. David's brothers went off to join the army; but David was too young and stayed at home.

One day David took some food to his brothers at the army camp. As he talked to his brothers, something extraordinary happened.

A huge giant named Goliath marched out from the Philistine camp. He was very, very tall and very, very strong.

"Who's brave enough to fight me?" the giant bellowed. "Haven't you Israelites got anyone brave enough to stand up to me?"

But the Israelites were very, very scared of the giant.

"*I* will go and fight Goliath," said young David. "Nobody else has volunteered."

"But you're just a boy," his brothers laughed.

So David went to King Saul.

"I'm not afraid of the giant," David told the king. "I will fight Goliath for you."

But King Saul said: "You're *much* too young!"

"I've killed a lion and a bear," said David. "God will help me fight this bold giant too."

"Go then!" said Saul. And he gave David

his very own armour. David put on the king's coat of mail and heavy helmet, and strapped on his huge sword.

"I can't even *walk* in these," said David, and took them all off again.

David went down to the brook and chose five smooth pebbles. He put them in his little shepherd's pouch. Then David walked out to meet Goliath.

Down the hillside strode the mighty giant. When he saw David, he bellowed with laughter.

"Is this the best you can find to fight me?" he yelled.

But David slipped a pebble quietly into his sling, whirled the sling around his head, and let fly. The stone struck Goliath right on his forehead – and the giant dropped down.

When the Philistines saw their strongest man fall dead, they all ran off.

Years later, after King Saul died, David became king of Israel, just as Samuel had promised.

1 Samuel chapter 17

Wisest of Kings

DAVID RULED AS KING of Israel for forty years. He had many sons, but it was his son Solomon who became king after David died.

David gave his son Solomon very good advice: "Be a strong king! Trust God, and obey his laws."

The people cheered when Solomon was crowned king of Israel.

After he became king, Solomon beat the armies of his father David's old enemies.

Solomon ruled the kingdom of Israel for many years, and became one of Israel's most famous kings. During his reign, the people of Israel lived in peace.

A wise request

One night, soon after he became king, God came to Solomon in a dream.

"What gift would you most like from me?" God asked.

"I'm still a young man and I rule a mighty nation," replied King Solomon. "Please, Lord, make me wise. I need to make good choices when my people come to me and ask what they should do."

God was pleased Solomon didn't just ask for riches.

"I will make you wiser than anyone who has ever lived," God promised the king.

So it was that Solomon became the wisest of kings.

Whose baby?

One day two women brought a baby to King Solomon's palace. They showed Solomon the baby.

"It's my baby!" shouted one woman.

"No it's not – it's mine!" yelled the other.

They were squabbling and shouting so noisily that Solomon had to call out, "Please stop all this noise! I cannot think!"

Now Solomon had to judge which of the two women was *really* mother of the baby.

He pondered long and hard.

Then the king commanded, "Call in the captain of my guards!"

When the captain arrived, Solomon ordered, "Take this little baby – and cut it in half! Then give these women half each!"

"No! No! *Please* don't do that!" one of the women shrieked. "*Please* don't hurt the baby! I'd rather this woman had the baby than that it was cut in two."

At once wise King Solomon knew this woman was the real mother. She truly loved the baby and wished above all that it lived. She had a true mother's love for the baby.

A Temple for God

King Solomon also set out to build a wonderful temple where the people could worship God.

The builders used huge stones to make the Temple walls. They brought fine wood such as cedar to make wall panels and furniture.

Solomon's Temple was to be a wonderful building, where the ark of the covenant – which contained the laws given to Moses – would be kept safely.

Finally the Temple was finished. At the back was a windowless room, called the Holiest Place, where the ark of the covenant stood. The walls of this room were covered in gold. No one ever entered, except the high priest, just once a year.

In an outer room stood a golden altar and ten golden lamp stands. Many other things in this wonderful Temple were also covered in gold, such as the tables, and the holy cups and bowls.

King Solomon made the Temple as fine as he could, and put the very best furnishings inside. Outside the Temple was a courtyard where the people could offer their gifts to God.

When the Temple was completed, Solomon held a special opening ceremony. The priests carried the ark of the covenant into the Temple. At once the Temple was filled with a dazzling, blinding light, to show that God was there with his people.

At the opening ceremony King Solomon prayed, "God of Israel, hear the prayers of your people. Listen to them and always help them."

After the ceremony, a great feast was held. It lasted a whole week!
1 Kings chapters 3, 6, 8

Elijah and the Wicked King

AFTER KING SOLOMON DIED, his kingdom split into two: the kingdom of Israel and the kingdom of Judah. Both kingdoms were sometimes ruled by good kings and sometimes by bad kings.

King Ahab was one of the very worst kings of Israel. He married a wicked woman called Jezebel and did many things that God said were wrong.

Ahab even let his people worship idols.

Elijah was one of God's special messengers; the Bible sometimes calls them "prophets". He told people what God thought about them.

God sent Elijah the prophet to teach King Ahab a lesson.

No rain!

"O Ahab, King of Israel," said Elijah. "You have done *so* many bad things that God says there will be no rain in your kingdom for many, many years!"

Naturally this made Ahab angry. In fact King Ahab was *so* angry that he wanted to harm Elijah.

Elijah ran away to hide in the desert. There he lived on his own, beside a little stream. He drank water from this brook.

But Elijah could find nothing to eat in the dry desert. So he prayed to God, asking for food. Soon after, God began to send big, black birds called ravens to Elijah, carrying meat for him in their beaks. In this way, Elijah had enough to eat.

But there was so little rain that one day even the little stream dried up. Now Elijah had nothing to drink. What was he to do?

No food!

"Lord, where shall I go to find food?" prayed Elijah.

"I will show you," God told him. "Start walking along the road back to Israel. On your way, you will meet a woman. You must ask this woman to give you something to eat."

Elijah did as God told him.

He set off on the road home.

And – just as God said – he met a woman by the roadside.

"Can you spare me some food?" Elijah asked the woman politely.

"But I only have enough food left for one last meal for me and my son," the woman told the prophet.

"Cook something for me first," Elijah told her. "If you do that, I promise there will *still* be enough for you and your son."

The woman did as Elijah told her. She cooked a meal for Elijah, and then prepared food for herself and her son.

And from that day on, this woman and her son never went without food.

Elijah meets the king again

Three long years passed with no rain.

Finally God said to Elijah, "Go back and see King Ahab again."

Elijah left the woman's house and went to King Ahab's palace, as God told him to.

"It's you, is it, Elijah?" said the king. "The troublemaker! I'm amazed you dare to come near my palace! You've brought nothing but trouble to my kingdom."

"Nonsense!" said Elijah. "And you know it! It's you, Ahab, who has brought all these troubles to your kingdom. You've done so many wrong things that God has punished you and your people. It's *your* fault there has been no rain all this time."

The king glowered at him. But in his heart, he knew Elijah was right.

"Now let's have a competition," Elijah went on. "Let's find out whose god is for real – your god Baal or my God."

Ahab agreed. So they both went to a hill called Mount Carmel to set up the contest.

King Ahab's prophets ran around collecting stones to build a fine altar for their god Baal. And Elijah found stones to build an altar for his God.

Then the contest began.

No answer!

First the king's prophets laid offerings on their altar made of stones. They prayed – and then waited for their god to answer their prayers, by sending fire to burn up the sacrifice.

Nothing happened!

The king's prophets screamed at their god Baal to send fire.

No fire came.

Elijah teased them. "Pray louder!" he called to them. "Perhaps your god is asleep. Perhaps he's out hunting and can't hear you!"

They shouted still louder. But nothing happened.

Finally they gave up.

By this time it was evening. God's prophet, Elijah, placed an offering on his altar. He poured water over the altar, to make it more difficult to catch fire.

Then Elijah prayed, "God in heaven, send fire on my altar."

And fire came. It burned up the offering, the stones, and even the water.

Now the people of Israel knew that Elijah's God was the true God – not King Ahab's god, Baal.

No escape!

Now at last God sent rain to Israel, after all those long, dry years.

But King Ahab and his horrible wife, Queen Jezebel, still wanted to have Elijah killed.

Elijah had to escape again to the desert. When he arrived there, he was so tired and miserable that he lay down and fell fast asleep.

Before long, someone tapped Elijah on his shoulder.

Elijah looked up startled. Had King Ahab's soldiers captured him? But no – it was an angel! The angel had come to cook Elijah a meal on the hot stones in the desert.

After a good dinner, Elijah felt strong enough to set off again on his long journey.

Then Elijah heard a gentle voice.

"Go and find a man named Elisha," it said. "He will help you – and do your job after you have gone."

It was the voice of God, telling Elijah he was no longer on his own.

He was going to have a helper!

1 Kings chapters 17–19

Elisha Helps a General

ELIJAH LEFT THE DESERT right away.

Soon he found Elisha, working in a field. Elijah placed his cloak over the young man's shoulders, to show that he wanted Elisha to become his helper.

Elisha said goodbye to his mother and father and followed God's prophet, Elijah.

By now Elijah was getting old. His young helper, Elisha, went with him everywhere.

Chariot of fire

One day Elijah and Elisha were walking along the road together, when all of a sudden a chariot and horses of fire appeared from nowhere. The fiery horses drove between the two men. Then *whoosh*! Elijah was carried up to heaven in this chariot of fire.

Elisha watched as he disappeared.

As Elijah flew upwards, his coat flew off and landed on the ground. Elisha picked it up thoughtfully. Now it would be his coat!

Then Elisha went on his way rather sadly.

Pots of oil

As he was walking through a little village one day, Elisha met a woman.

"I have nothing to eat!" she said. "Just this one tiny pot of oil."

"Borrow as many empty pots and jars as you can from your friends," Elisha told the woman. "Take them all home, then pour your oil into them."

It seemed an odd thing to do – but the woman trusted God's prophet.

She went off around her village, begging and borrowing from her friends. Soon she'd collected up lots and lots of jars, pots, jugs, pitchers, bowls, and bottles. She carried them all home.

Then the woman started to pour out the oil from her own pot. She poured and poured and poured. The oil just kept coming. Soon she'd filled every last jar in the house.

Then the woman took her jars, pots, jugs, pitchers, bowls, and bottles full of oil to market. She set up a little stall and sold her oil.

Soon she'd earned enough money to pay off everything she owed.

And she had enough money left over to buy plenty of food for her family.

The boy who sneezed

Another woman also begged Elisha for help.

"My little boy has died," she cried. "*Please* help me!"

Elisha went straight to her house and prayed for her son.

The little boy sneezed and opened his eyes.

He had come back to life!

The general with skin disease

Naaman, a very important general in the army, had a horrible skin disease called leprosy. Men and women with leprosy were not allowed to get close to other people. They had to live in separate villages.

Naaman's wife had a young servant girl.

"I do wish my master could meet the prophet Elisha," said the girl. "Elisha's God could help him."

When Naaman heard this, he asked the girl about the prophet, and where he could find him. Then Naaman and his guards set off from his fine house to find the prophet Elisha.

Elisha lived in a simple cottage in a little village. He was very surprised to see the proud general and his guards at his door.

"I have a horrid skin disease," explained Naaman. "My servant girl told me you might be able to help me."

Elisha said something quite strange.

"Go and wash in the River Jordan seven times," he told Naaman. "After that, you'll be completely well again."

Naaman wasn't at all sure about this. He was a proud general – and what Elisha was telling him to do seemed rather silly.

The Jordan was a dirty, muddy river. How would washing in such mucky water help?

"Master – do as the prophet says!" urged Naaman's servants.

So Naaman decided to go along with what Elisha said.

He went to the River Jordan to wash.

Naaman dipped himself in the river – once, twice, three times…

And after the seventh time, the leprosy vanished! Naaman's skin was as smooth and clear as a newborn baby's.

Elisha's God had healed him.

2 Kings chapter 5

Daniel, the King, and the Lions

DARIUS THE GREAT was king of the Medes and the Persians.

He was a mighty king – and he had one hundred and twenty governors to help him rule his huge kingdom.

Daniel was one of the king's governors. Daniel came from the kingdom of Judah. He was Jewish: he didn't worship the gods of the Medes and the Persians.

Every morning, every lunchtime, and every night before he went to bed, Daniel prayed to the living God.

Daniel was particularly wise. He gave the king excellent advice and King Darius trusted him.

Daniel did so well that Darius chose him to become one of his three top governors.

And Daniel became so good at *this* job that Darius decided to put him in charge of his *whole* kingdom.

All the other governors were furious. Why did the king always listen to Daniel? And anyway Daniel was a foreigner. How come he got the very top job?

All the other governors tried their hardest to find some fault in Daniel – but they couldn't.

Daniel was just too good. The king could always trust him: Daniel never did anything wrong.

91

A trap for Daniel

So the jealous governors hatched a plot against Daniel.

One day they went to the king.

"O King Darius, live forever!" said the governors. "You alone are wise and powerful."

The king liked what he was hearing.

"Yes – I'm very wise and powerful," he thought.

"O King, make a new law!" one of the governors continued. "A new law that says no one must pray to anyone except *you*!"

The king liked this too!

"And if anyone disobeys this law," added another governor jumping with excitement, "he or she will be thrown into a pit full of lions."

The king puffed out his chest. This all sounded great!

"Write down this new law for me," Darius told his governors.

The governors did as he said – and then the king pressed his seal into the wax on the scroll they gave him. Now it was official – it had become royal law.

The new law was proclaimed by trumpeters throughout Darius the Great's kingdom.

"This is the law of the Medes and Persians," the messengers said. "It cannot be changed. No one must pray to anyone except King Darius!"

Sneaks!

Now the jealous governors took the next step in their plot. They hid themselves where they could spy on Daniel's house.

That very lunchtime, the governors

watched Daniel enter his house. They saw him go to his window. He got down on his knees and prayed to God – just as he did every other day.

The governors rushed back to King Darius.

"O King, live forever!" they gasped. "Did you not order that nobody should pray to any god except you?"

"Yes, of course I did!" said Darius.

"Have you not ordered that anyone who disobeys this law will be thrown to the lions?"

"Yes, of course I have!" said Darius again.

"Well – we've seen with our own eyes. Daniel is still praying to his God," they sneaked.

"Oh dear!" said Darius the Great. "Oh dear! *Oh dear!*"

"Every morning, every lunchtime, and every night before he goes to bed, Daniel prays to God," the jealous governors announced to the king.

They felt so pleased with themselves.

"Oh dear," said the king yet again. "What am I to do?"

Darius the Great was really very sorry, because he liked and respected Daniel.

He tried to think of some way that he could save his top governor.

"The law of the Medes and Persians cannot be changed," the governors reminded the king. "Daniel *must* be thrown into the lions' pit."

So, very sadly, the foolish king had to agree.

Soldiers soon marched Daniel before King Darius.

"Daniel must be thrown into the pit of lions," ordered the king.

Then he added in a softer voice, "May his God help him!"

Into the pit

Immediately, soldiers seized Daniel and threw him into the pit of lions, just outside Darius the Great's palace.

The soldiers rolled a stone across the entrance to the pit. Then King Darius stuck his seal on the stone. Now no one could rescue Daniel.

That night, back in his palace, the king could not eat and could not sleep. He couldn't stop thinking about poor Daniel in the pit of lions.

As soon as morning came, Darius leapt out of bed and rushed straight down to the lions' pit.

"Daniel!" he called down. "Are you there? Are you all right?"

To the king's huge surprise, there stood Daniel – whole and unharmed.

"O King, live forever!" said Daniel. "I'm here and I'm fine. Not a scratch!"

"But Daniel – how come you're not hurt?" called Darius.

"During the night, God sent an angel to shut the mouths of the lions – so they couldn't bite me," Daniel explained. "God knew I'd done nothing wrong. He answered my prayers."

King Darius was overjoyed.

"Get Daniel out of the pit!" he shouted. "Set him free at once!"

Once Daniel was free, Darius ordered his soldiers, "Go, arrest all those wicked governors who trapped Daniel!"

Then Darius the Great ordered his people: "From this day, everyone must respect Daniel's God. He is the living God. He saved Daniel from the lions. *This* is the law of the Medes and Persians. It cannot be changed!"
Daniel chapter 6

Jonah and the Great Big Fish

ONE DAY GOD SPOKE to his prophet Jonah.

"Go to the great city of Nineveh!" God said. "Tell the people there they are *very* bad – and I'm going to punish them."

"I don't want to go to Nineveh and tell them God's going to punish them," thought Jonah. "That's much too scary!"

So Jonah ran away instead.

Jonah went to the seaport, paid his fare, and got on a ship going in the opposite direction to Nineveh.

Soon the ship sailed off, taking Jonah farther and farther away from the great city of Nineveh.

A great storm

Before long God sent a terrifying storm.

The waves rose higher and higher, the rain fell, and lightning flashed. It was soon so rough that the ship almost broke in two.

The sailors were very frightened!

"God, help us!" they cried out. "Don't let us all drown!"

Meanwhile Jonah was sprawled out snoring below deck. He hadn't even noticed the storm!

The captain clambered down to the bottom of the ship to find Jonah.

"Wake up!" he shouted. "Help us pray! Perhaps God will listen to *you*!

Jonah woke up startled.

"God won't hear me," he told the captain. "This is all my fault, because I disobeyed God. I shouldn't be on your ship at all. I'm supposed to be in Nineveh. That's why God sent the storm."

Jonah climbed up on deck with the captain. The ship was rocking and rolling. It felt as if any minute it might capsize.

"Throw me into the sea!" Jonah yelled to the sailors. "Perhaps then the storm will stop – and you will be safe."

At first the sailors didn't want to, but the storm was becoming wilder and wilder.

So, with a huge heave, the sailors tossed Jonah overboard into the sea.

The moment Jonah hit the water, the storm stopped!

A great fish

Down, down into the swirling water went Jonah. He was sure he was going to drown.

Then all of a sudden – *gulp*! Something swallowed Jonah whole.

He was inside the stomach of a huge,

great, big, enormous, gigantic fish that was swimming past.

Jonah stayed in the tummy of that fish for three whole days and three nights!

"Lord, save me!" he prayed from the fish's tummy.

He was more scared now than he had been when God told him to go to Nineveh.

And more scared even than in the storm.

But God had heard Jonah praying.

On the third day, the huge, great, big, enormous, gigantic fish spat Jonah out onto the seashore.

Jonah stood up, shook off the seaweed, dried himself down, and wondered what to do next.

Then God spoke to Jonah again.

"Go to the great city of Nineveh!" God said. "Say to the bad people there: 'God is going to punish you.'"

This time Jonah did what God said.

He went to Nineveh. He told the people there, "God is going to destroy your great city. It will stand for only forty more days!"

A great change

The people of Nineveh were very frightened.

They knelt down.

"We're so sorry!" they prayed. "Forgive us! We want to change."

And God heard them.

"I've decided I won't destroy your city after all," God told the people of Nineveh.

So the ship was saved. Jonah was saved. And the city of Nineveh was saved too!

Jonah chapters 1–3

Jesus is Born

THERE WAS A YOUNG WOMAN called Mary who lived in the little town of Nazareth.

One day an angel visited her.

Mary was amazed – and a bit frightened.

"Mary!" said the angel. "There's no need to be worried."

Immediately Mary felt much happier.

"My name is Gabriel. I bring great news for you, from God your heavenly Father!" the angel continued. "You are going to have a baby. You must call him Jesus. God is sending him to save the world."

Now Mary was puzzled.

"How can this happen?" she asked. "I'm not even married."

She could hardly believe what she was hearing.

"God will make this happen," said the angel. "With God *nothing* is impossible."

When she heard this, Mary was filled with joy.

"I will do whatever God wants," she said.

As she spoke, the angel disappeared.

A long journey

Mary loved a kind and good man called Joseph, the village carpenter. Mary and Joseph were engaged to be married.

Soon after Gabriel's visit, Joseph had a dream. In his dream an angel told him, "Joseph, you need to look after Mary."

So Mary and Joseph got married straight away.

It was nearly time for Mary's baby to be born when one day some soldiers nailed up a notice in the village.

It said: "Everyone must go back to the town where they were born, to register their name."

So Joseph and Mary had to go to Joseph's home town, Bethlehem, many miles away.

Mary and Joseph set out on the long journey to Bethlehem. Mary rode their little donkey and Joseph walked alongside. They slept where they could, wrapped in their warm coats.

"Are we nearly there?" said Mary, "I'm so tired. I just want to lie down and rest."

"Look – there are the lights of Bethlehem!" said Joseph, pointing ahead. "We'll soon be there now."

By the time Mary and Joseph had climbed the hill to Bethlehem, it was already dark.

"How will we ever find somewhere to stay?" asked Mary. "There are so many people."

Lots of other people had also come to the town to register their names.

"We'll try to find a room," said Joseph.

They stopped at an inn and he knocked on the door.

When a man came out, Joseph asked: "Can you let us have a room?"

"No, I'm sorry!" the innkeeper shook his head. "We're completely full. There's not a bed to be had in the whole town."

As he was speaking, the innkeeper caught sight of Mary's tired face.

"There is a little stable where my animals sleep," he added. "You and your wife could sleep there. It's the best I can offer, I'm afraid. But you're most welcome to it!"

He showed Mary and Joseph the stable. The animals had made it feel quite warm.

The two tired visitors decided to spend the night there, in the simple stable. Joseph unpacked their things.

Mary lay down in the straw.

Mary's baby is born

There in the stable, among the donkeys and cows, Mary's baby was born. Mary held him close and looked at him lovingly.

The oxen watched too.

And Joseph's little donkey.

Mary wrapped her baby around and around in a long piece of soft cloth, to keep him warm.

"Joseph – we don't have a cradle for our baby," said Mary.

So Joseph put clean straw in the animals' feed box.

"I've made a bed for baby Jesus in the cows' manger," he said.

Joseph laid the baby gently in the manger, and Jesus soon fell fast asleep on the straw.

The shepherds' visit

It was dark in the fields outside Bethlehem.

But the shepherds were still awake, making sure their sheep were safe.

All of a sudden, a piercing, bright light shone down. Everything was lit up.

"What's that light!" asked one shepherd, trembling.

All the shepherds were scared.

"Don't look now," said another, very frightened. "There's an angel!"

"There's no need to be afraid," said the angel. "I have good news that will bring joy to all people."

The shepherds listened in wonder.

"Today your king has been born in Bethlehem," the angel went on. "You will find him lying in a manger. Go – see for yourselves!"

Then suddenly a whole crowd of angels

filled the sky, singing, "Glory to God on high, and peace to his people on earth!"

Then the light faded and the night became quiet once again.

Now the shepherds started to talk.

"We've seen angels!"

"You heard what the angel said – a king has been born. Tonight – here in Bethlehem!"

"Let's see if we can find him!"

"Come on!"

And they rushed off into Bethlehem to look for the baby king, leaving their sheep on the hillside.

Soon the shepherds found the innkeeper's stable. They peered inside and saw Mary, Joseph, and baby Jesus lying in a manger.

They crowded in to look at the baby, trying not to wake him. Then the shepherds knelt down.

They told Mary and Joseph excitedly what the angel had told them. Everyone was astonished.

Then, noticing that Mary was tired, the shepherds crept out again and went back to look after their sheep.

But Mary kept thinking about everything they had said.

Luke 1:26–38,
2:1–20

Wise Men Seek a New King

IN A FARAWAY LAND in the East lived some very wise men. They studied old books by day, and by night they watched the stars.

Late one evening one of the wise men exclaimed excitedly, "I've never seen that star before!"

"It's new!" said a second, coming to look.

"This star is a sign," said a third wise man, who had read about it in his books. "A new king has been born!"

"Then we must follow this star, and find the new king," they all agreed.

So the wise men set out on a long journey, following the bright, new star.

After crossing deserts and wastelands, hills and valleys, the star led the wise men at last to Jerusalem, to the palace of King Herod.

Where is the king?

"O Herod, mighty King of the Jews! Where can we find the newborn king?" asked the wise men. "We have seen his star in the East, and we have come to worship him."

When King Herod heard this, he was angry.

"I'm the king around here," he thought. "I don't want a new king who might steal my crown!"

So Herod called for his top advisers.

"Have you heard anything about a new king?" he asked them. "If so, where will he be born?"

The advisers scurried off to look in their ancient books.

"Your Majesty," the king's advisers explained when they returned, "our holy books say the new king will be born in the town of Bethlehem."

So Herod summoned the wise men again.

"Go and seek out this child!" Herod told them. "When you find him, come back and tell me where he is. I would *love* to go and worship him too."

But Herod was lying. He really wanted to harm the baby when he found him. He didn't want anyone else claiming to be king of *his* country!

Now the star led the wise men once more. It went ahead of them until it stopped over the house in Bethlehem where Jesus was.

Gifts for a baby

The wise men entered the house.

Inside they found young Jesus with his mother, Mary.

When the wise men saw Jesus, they knelt down before him. They had brought with them rich presents: gold, and precious scents called frankincense and myrrh. They gave them to the little boy.

They were presents fit for a king.

But that same night God sent a warning to the wise men in a dream.

"Don't go back to see King Herod!" an angel told them. "He wants to harm the baby when he discovers where he is."

So the wise men did not return to Herod's palace in Jerusalem. They journeyed home a different way.

After the wise men left, Joseph had a dream too.

"Get up – now!" an angel told him. "Take little Jesus and his mother, and flee to Egypt. King Herod is looking for the baby and wants to harm him. Stay in Egypt until I tell you it's safe to return home."

So Joseph got up in the middle of the night. He woke Mary and they set off for Egypt, taking little Jesus with them.

There they stayed until King Herod was dead, and it was safe to return.

Matthew 2:1–14

Lost in Jerusalem

MARY, JOSEPH, AND JESUS stayed in the land of Egypt until they heard it was safe to return home.

Then they set out on the long journey to Nazareth, where Mary and Joseph lived before Jesus was born.

At last they saw little houses in the distance. There was the town of Nazareth, nestling among the hills.

Jesus grew up with Mary and Joseph in Nazareth. Joseph worked as a carpenter, and Jesus often helped in his workshop, sawing and hammering.

Sometimes Jesus played with the other children. Sometimes he helped the shepherds look after their sheep. Sometimes he helped the women fetch water from the old well.

When he was old enough, Jesus started school. He learned to read. He listened carefully to the lessons and remembered what he was taught. How proud his mother Mary felt!

Big laws and little laws

Jesus also learned about God's laws. Jewish teachers had written down the Law of God. There were little laws and big laws. The little laws told people exactly how they should wash a plate, arrange their clothes, and what things they shouldn't eat.

When Jesus saw that people sometimes thought more about doing these little things right than about big things, such as being kind to one another, he was puzzled.

"Surely it's better to be like old Sarah, who lives next door and is always kind to everyone, though she sometimes forgets the little rules, than it is to be like James, who never forgets these little things, but is unfair and unkind," thought Jesus.

Once a year the Jewish people had a great holiday festival. They liked to go to Jerusalem, where the great Temple stood. Joseph and Mary loved to go too.

When Jesus was twelve years old, Mary said to him, "This year you can come with us to the festival in Jerusalem. You're a big boy now, and you've learned the Law of God well. It's time you came to the Temple with us."

A great festival

It was an exciting journey over the hills and plains to Jerusalem. Some of Jesus' friends came too. Each day brought interesting new sights. At night they lit campfires, cooked supper, and sang. It was all great fun!

At last they neared Jerusalem. From the hills outside, the visitors could see the whole city, and the great Temple gleaming white and gold in the sunlight.

Once they had found somewhere to stay during the festival, Mary, Joseph, and Jesus went to the Temple. Jesus looked at the amazing, tall building.

"This is the house of God, my heavenly Father," he thought. "I'm going to his house."

In the Temple, Jesus met wise men and priests. They made him a follower of God's Law.

"He's sure to come and look for us when we set up camp tonight," she said to Joseph.

But night came – and still there was no sign of Jesus.

"We must search for him, Joseph," said Mary, anxiously. "Go and ask the other boys if they know where our Jesus is."

"No!" said the boys when Joseph asked them. "We haven't seen Jesus all day either."

Mary is worried

Nobody had seen Jesus since they left Jerusalem. Now Mary and Joseph were really worried.

"We have to return to Jerusalem," said Joseph.

So back they went.

But they *still* couldn't find Jesus.

For three days Joseph and Mary walked up and down the bustling, narrow streets of the great city.

They asked everyone they met, "Have you seen our boy, Jesus?"

"There's only one place left to look," said Mary at last, with a sigh. "In the Temple itself. Jesus loved visiting the Temple, Joseph. Perhaps he's gone back there."

They went to look – and there, just as Mary guessed, they found Jesus. He'd been in the Temple all the time!

Jesus had found the wise men again. They knew more about the Jewish Law than anyone else he had met.

"Now you must behave as a grown-up," they said. "You must try to keep all God's laws."

Too soon, the great holiday festival was over. It was time to go home.

"How nice it's been to meet all our old friends!" said Mary. "But it will be great to get home to our own little house."

They started the long walk back to Nazareth. Mary didn't see Jesus all that day.

Jesus had been asking questions – questions that even these learned men didn't always know how to answer!

The old men were astonished that this young Jewish boy knew so much about the Law of God.

Jesus had stayed there for hours, asking questions, and sometimes answering the holy men's questions too.

He'd forgotten about everything else: now at last he was finding out about things he needed to know.

Jesus is found

Then Jesus saw Joseph and Mary looking for him anxiously.

Mary went to him, almost in tears.

"Jesus, my son!" she said. "Why did you do this? Your father and I have been looking for you everywhere. We've been *so* worried."

Jesus was surprised.

"But didn't you guess I'd be here?" he asked. "I had to come to my Father's house, to learn the things I need to know about."

This time Jesus did set off for home with Mary and Joseph. When they arrived, he settled down again in Nazareth, helping his father and mother, as he'd always done.

But Jesus often thought back to what he had learned during those special days with the wise men in the Temple.

Luke 2:41–52

John Baptizes Jesus

JOHN WAS DIFFERENT.

He lived in the desert. He wore clothes made of rough camel's hair, tied with a leather belt. He lived on food he found in the desert – wild honey and insects called locusts.

God had given John a special job to do.

John went to people and said, "You do a lot of bad things. You don't live as God would like you to. Turn around and start doing what's right."

"How can we make a fresh start?" people asked him.

"Have you got two shirts?" John asked in reply. "If so, give one to someone who doesn't have *any* shirts!"

People were a bit surprised when he said this sort of thing.

"Have you got enough to eat?" he asked sometimes. "Then share your food with someone who's hungry!"

Crowds of people flocked to hear John speaking.

Many of them said they *were* sorry for the wrong things they'd done.

"God wants to forgive you when you've done wrong," he told them.

John dipped them in the River Jordan. He

'baptized' them. When they came out of the water, they felt as if they were making a fresh start.

People used to call him "John the Baptizer" or "John the Baptist".

A dove appears

Some people asked John: "Are you the one God is sending to save us?"

"Soon, someone much *greater* than me will come," John told them. "I'm not fit even to undo his sandals!"

One day, soon after this, Jesus came to John beside the River Jordan.

"Please baptize me," Jesus said to John.

"But Jesus, I should be baptized by you," said John. "There's no way I should be baptizing you!"

"This is the way God wants it!" Jesus replied.

So John agreed.

He dipped Jesus in the River Jordan.

When Jesus came out of the water, a dove appeared over his head.

Then a voice from heaven said: "This is my own dear son. I am very pleased with him."

Matthew chapter 3

Jesus Chooses His Team

ONE DAY JESUS was standing on the shore of Lake Galilee. Lots of people crowded around him, listening to him telling his wonderful stories.

Jesus noticed two fishing boats on the beach. The fishermen were washing their nets. Jesus climbed into one of the boats. It belonged to a man called Simon Peter.

"Push the boat out a little way from the shore," he told Simon Peter.

Then Jesus talked to the people from Simon Peter's boat.

When he had finished teaching the crowd, Jesus said to Simon Peter, "Push out into deeper water and let down your nets, so you can catch plenty of fish."

"But, Master," Simon Peter answered, "we've been hard at work all night – and we've not caught a single fish. However, if you say so, I'll let down the nets again."

This time the fishermen's nets were soon so full of fish that they began to rip.

They called to their friends in the other boat to help them.

Before long both boats were so full of fish that they nearly sank.

Simon Peter, his brother Andrew, and their fishermen friends, the twins James and John, were amazed to see so many fish.

Simon Peter went and knelt before Jesus. "Leave me, Lord! I am a sinful man," he said.

"Don't be scared!" Jesus told him. "From now on you'll be fishing for people."

So the fishermen pulled their boats up the beach, left everything, and followed Jesus.

They became the first of Jesus' special followers, the 'disciples'.

Special friends

People didn't like tax collectors.

They cheated people and took too much money. They were thieves!

One day Jesus saw a taxman called Matthew working at his desk.

"Follow me!" he called over to him.

At once Matthew got up, left his work and his money, and followed Jesus. He became one of Jesus' special friends.

Then Jesus called more men to be his special followers: Philip, Bartholomew, Thomas the twin, another James, Thaddaeus, another Simon, and Judas Iscariot.

There were twelve altogether. They became Jesus' special friends, the disciples.
Luke 5:1–11, 27–32; 6:12–16

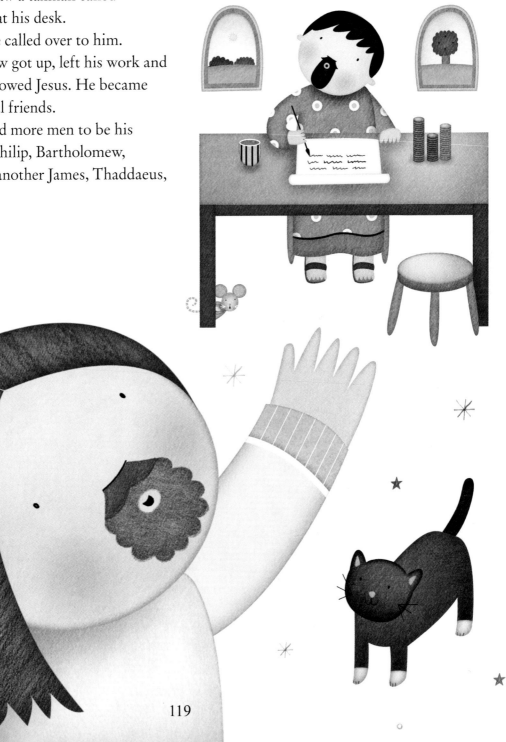

119

Our Father

JESUS OFTEN WENT up into the hills around Galilee.

One day, a crowd gathered there to hear him teaching and telling stories.

He explained to them about the good things God does for us:

"Happy are those who want to do God's wishes.

"Forgive others and you will be forgiven.

"People with pure hearts will see God.

"People who work for peace are God's children.

"If you are ill-treated for doing what God asks, be happy, for your reward is in heaven."

Salt and light

Jesus used picture language to help people understand his teachings more easily.

"You are like salt that we put in our food to stop it going off," he told them. "You will keep God's world from going bad.

"Your good deeds are like lamps shining in the darkness, lighting up God's world. People will thank God for them.

"God has given you special laws. You must always follow them.

"God says, 'You shall not murder.' But it's also wrong to feel so angry that you want to hurt someone.

"God says, 'Love your enemies and be kind to those who do us wrong.'"

How to pray

One of Jesus' friends asked, "Lord, how should we pray?"

So Jesus taught them how to pray:

"Go somewhere quiet when you want to pray to God. He knows exactly what you need.

"And this is how you should pray to him:

"Our Father in heaven,
May your holy name be respected;
May your kingdom come;
May your will be done on earth,
*   as it is in heaven.*
Give us today, the food we need.
Forgive us the wrongs we have done,
As we forgive the wrongs
*   that others have done to us.*
Do not bring us to the point of temptation,
But keep us safe from evil."

Matthew 5:1–20, 6:5–15

Jesus Helps a Little Girl

THERE WAS A LITTLE GIRL who lived in the fishing village of Capernaum, beside the Lake of Galilee. Her father was called Jairus.

One day the little girl woke up feeling unwell.

"My head hurts," she complained. "I don't feel like having any breakfast. And I don't much want to play."

The doctor came, but the girl felt no better.

Two or three days later, the girl was feeling really ill.

Her father, Jairus, was very worried.

"Have you heard about this new healer, the man called Jesus?" he asked his wife. "I think he's here in Capernaum."

"Do you think you can find him?" said his wife. "Perhaps he'll come and help our daughter."

"I'll try!" said Jairus. "I've heard he's a good man who loves children. I'm sure he'd come to see our little girl."

Jairus rushed out of the house and into the town. Anxiously he asked people where he might find Jesus.

He went to the house where Jesus usually stayed – but he wasn't there.

"Go down to the lake," said the woman who opened the door. "He might be teaching at the lakeside."

Is Jesus here?

So Jairus hurried down to the beach, where he could see a crowd of people.

"Is Jesus here?" asked Jairus anxiously.

"No, he's not!" said a fisherman. "He was here last night, telling us stories from the fisherman's boat. Then he sailed off across the lake."

"We're waiting for his boat to return," said another man.

"Do you think he'll be long?" asked Jairus, in despair.

Nobody seemed to know.

All at once someone shouted, "Look! I can see a boat now... Jesus is coming!"

Minutes later, the fishing boat ran up on the shore. Jesus jumped out onto the sandy beach. His friends tried to keep back the people who were crowding around.

"Let me get through!" begged Jairus. "Please let me through!"

The crowd let him pass. They could see he wanted to say something important to Jesus.

Jairus begged Jesus to come and see his little girl.

"She's terribly ill," said Jairus, his voice a bit wobbly. "Please come, so she'll be healed."

Jesus saw Jairus was very worried.

"I'll come at once," he said. "Let's go!"

They set off. Then Jairus saw a man pushing through the people.

"Where's Jairus?" asked the man.

Too late?

Jairus's heart went cold.

"Sir!" said the messenger. "Don't bother Jesus now. Your little girl has died."

It was too late!

"Don't be afraid!" Jesus said gently. "Just believe in me."

Jesus walked on with Jairus, and the crowd followed.

When they were quite near Jairus's house, Jesus turned around and said to the people following, "Don't come any further!"

Taking just his close friends James, Peter, and John, Jesus went into the house with Jairus.

As soon as they were inside, they heard a lot of weeping and wailing.

"Please go away!" said Jesus to the people making all the noise. "The little girl isn't dead – she's asleep."

But they laughed at him.

Jesus sent them off anyway, and followed Jairus into the room where the little girl lay.

Wake up!

The girl's mother stood there weeping.

"You're too late, Jairus!" she sobbed.

Jesus stood by the bed, looking at the child. He took the little girl's hand gently in his warm hands.

"My dear, wake up!" Jesus said.

The little girl opened her eyes. Then she sat up and looked around.

She was astonished to see so many people in the room. She smiled at her father.

The girl's father and mother kissed and hugged her, crying for joy.

"Find your dear girl something to eat," said Jesus.

Once the little girl had eaten some food and had a drink, she felt much better. Then Jesus left.

Jairus's family never forgot that wonderful day when their little girl was brought back to life.

Luke 8:40–42, 49–56

The Boy With Loaves and Fishes for Lunch

woman. "He sailed off in his boat across the lake with his friends. So we walked around the lake to try to find him."

"Who's Jesus?" asked the little boy.

"Haven't you heard about him?" a girl asked. "He's a wonderful man. He can do miracles! And tell great stories. That's why I've come today – I love stories."

"So do I," said the little boy. "I wish I could see this man and hear some of his stories. I'll go and ask my mother if I can come too."

THERE WAS ONCE a little boy who lived with his mother and father in a house near Lake Galilee.

One day he was out on the hills when he saw lots of people walking by. Where were they all going?

The boy ran towards the crowd.

"Why are you all coming past?" he asked.

"We're looking for Jesus," said a friendly

Stories and miracles

So he ran off home.

"Mother! Have you heard of a man called Jesus?" asked the boy. "He tells stories and does miracles. Can I go and hear him? I do *so* want to see him."

"Of course you can!" said his mother, smiling. "Just wait while I pack up some food for you. Look, here are five little loaves and two fish."

The boy could hardly wait for his mother to put the food into a basket for him. Then he said goodbye and ran off.

By the time he arrived, the crowds had grown even bigger.

"Is Jesus here yet?" he asked anxiously.

"He's over there, on the hillside," said a man. "His friends are with him."

Jesus had come to the hills for a rest, because he was tired. But when he saw the crowds of people, he felt sorry for them.

Jesus' friends started to walk among the crowd, looking for sick and disabled people to take to Jesus. The boy saw Jesus put his hands on the people who were ill and talk to them. Suddenly they were well again. They could see, they could walk and run again! They went away, thanking God.

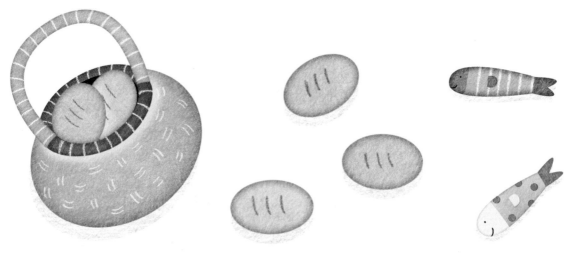

No shops!

After this, Jesus sat down and started to tell the people some of his wonderful stories. The boy listened carefully, so he wouldn't miss a word Jesus said.

"What great stories!" he thought. "I'll remember every one of them to tell mother and father tonight. They'd love to hear them."

The boy forgot all about the food in his little basket.

The day went on, and before long the sun began to set. Hundreds of people were still out there on the hills, excited and happy.

But by now they were beginning to feel a bit tired. And hungry. They hadn't brought any food with them – and there were no shops in the hills.

Some of Jesus' friends went to him.

"Master!" they said. "Shall we send these people away to the villages to buy bread?"

"No – we must feed them here," said Jesus.

"But Master, it would cost a lot to buy food for all these people," said Jesus' friend Philip, who looked after the money for Jesus. "Do you seriously want us to go off and buy food for them?"

"Hasn't *anyone* here got food?" asked Jesus. "Go and find out."

No food?

So Jesus' friends went around the hillside asking, "Has anyone brought some food with them?"

Everyone shook their heads.

Then the little boy heard one of the disciples asking, "Who has food?"

Suddenly he remembered his basket of food – five little loaves and two small fish.

"I would love to give them to Jesus," he thought.

So the boy pushed his way through the crowds of people and went up to one of Jesus' friends.

"I have a little bread," he said. "And look – two small fish as well. You can have them."

The man led the boy to Jesus.

"Master!" he said. "Here's a boy with five

loaves and two little fish."

Jesus smiled at the boy and took his basket.

"Get everyone to sit down in groups," Jesus told his friends.

The little boy watched.

What would Jesus do next?

Jesus took the little loaves from the boy's basket and broke them. He thanked God for the bread. Then he gave it to his friends.

Next Jesus divided the little fish and gave the pieces to his friends as well.

Jesus' friends started to give the food to the great crowd of people sitting on the hillside.

To the little boy's astonishment, Jesus always seemed to have more for them. Jesus went on and on, breaking up the bread and fish, giving out more and more.

"There seems to be no end to my bread and fish!" thought the boy. "How can so little become so much? Jesus must be doing one of his miracles!"

Lots of leftovers

There were more than five thousand people sitting on the hillside – and every one of them had enough to eat.

When they had all eaten as much as they wanted, Jesus asked his friends to pick up all the leftovers. He wanted no crumbs left behind to litter the green hillside.

The little boy counted the baskets filled with leftovers.

"Twelve!" he said. "Twelve baskets full of scraps. And yet I only brought one little basket of food. This really is a wonderful miracle!"

By now it was time for everyone to start the journey home. The sun had set and it would soon be dark.

The boy ran home along the hillside paths.

"Mother, I saw Jesus!" he called as he burst into his house. "And do you know what happened to the five little loaves and the two fish you gave me? Jesus took them and – Mother, would you believe it? – there was enough to feed more than five thousand people! I saw a miracle done with my own bread and fish!

"I shall never forget today," the boy said. "It's been the best day of my life!"

Luke 9:10–17

Jesus Stops a Storm

JESUS WAS WITH his special friends, the disciples, beside Lake Galilee.

Many people had come to listen to him. Jesus had been telling some of his wonderful stories.

When evening came, Jesus said to his friends, "Come on, let's go across to the other side of the lake."

So Jesus and his disciples said goodbye to the people who'd been listening and got into their boat. They set off to sail across the water.

Jesus was very tired. He'd been talking to crowds of people all day and needed a rest.

Once he was in the boat, Jesus lay his head on a pillow and went to sleep.

Suddenly, a fierce wind blew down from the hills surrounding the lake. The disciples were caught in a storm!

Shipwreck?

Huge waves splashed all around and the boat began to rock.

Heavy rain fell.

The boat was tossed backwards and forwards. It began to fill with water.

By now the disciples were very scared. They knew how dangerous a storm on the lake could be.

But Jesus was still sleeping peacefully.

The disciples decided to rouse him.

"Master, wake up!" they shouted. "*Please do something to save us – or we're all going to drown!*"

Jesus awoke. He stood up.

"Be still!" he said firmly to the wind and the waves.

At that instant the wind dropped. The waves calmed. Everything was still.

Jesus turned back to his disciples, "Why were you so frightened?" he asked. "I am with you. You can always trust me."

"Where does Jesus get such power?" the friends asked each other.

"Even the wind and the waves do what he tells them!"

Mark 4:35–41

The Stranger Who Helped

JESUS TOLD MANY wonderful stories. They usually had a special meaning.

Here is one of Jesus' best-loved stories.

There was once a man who had to travel from Jerusalem to Jericho along a lonely road through the mountains.

He packed his bags and set out early. But the road got steeper and the sun hotter.

The man dared not stop, for fear he wouldn't arrive in Jericho before nightfall.

So he plodded on.

Some robbers hiding behind rocks saw him coming. Before the man knew what was happening, the robbers leapt on him.

Help!

He tried to beat off the robbers, but there were too many of them. They grabbed his bags and ripped off his best coat.

The robbers stole everything he had and then beat him up. They ran off, leaving him injured on the ground.

The man lay on the road. He was too badly hurt to walk and his head ached.

What was he to do? All he could hear was chirruping grasshoppers.

Then he heard a new sound – *flip-flop, flip-flop*. The man tried to lift his head.

Yes! It was a priest walking to Jerusalem. Surely he would help!

"Help!" the man called out feebly. "Help! Help!"

But when the priest saw the man lying on the ground, he just turned up his nose.

The priest didn't stop. He crossed to the opposite side of the road and walked on.

Flip-flop, flip-flop. The sound of his sandals soon disappeared into the distance.

The injured man couldn't believe anyone would be so heartless.

He lay still again. The sun beat down.

Then he heard *clomp-clomp, clomp-clomp.*

Yes! It was someone else on their way to Jerusalem.

He saw it was one of the men who helped in the Temple. Surely *he* would help!

The injured man called out again, "Help! Please help!"

The Temple helper looked around in fright. As soon as he saw the injured man in the road, he crossed over and started to walk faster! Straight past the injured man. He was scared the robbers might attack him too.

A stranger!

By this time the sun was sinking in the sky. No one else would be coming down the road now. It was much too dangerous in the dark.

The man lay very still.

Then he heard a faint *clip-clop, clip-clop* of a donkey. It got closer.

Now the injured man could see it was a foreigner. A man from Samaria, a "Samaritan". The Jews and the Samaritans were enemies.

"I've always heard Samaritans are mean and selfish," he thought to himself. "This man won't help me. He probably won't even stop."

But when the foreigner reached the injured man, he shouted "Whoa!" to his donkey and walked across.

"What's happened here?" he asked kindly. "You look in a bad way."

"I set out to walk to Jericho this morning," explained the injured man. "But robbers beat me up and took everything I had. I can hardly stand up. I've been lying here all day."

Strapped to the donkey's back were some bottles of oil. The Samaritan fetched them and rubbed olive oil gently into the man's wounds. Then he bandaged them with strips of clean cloth.

"Are you feeling a bit better now?" he asked. "Can you get on my donkey, if I give you a hand? You ride, and I'll steady you while I walk alongside."

The Samaritan helped the injured man climb on the donkey's back.

It was dark now and the stars were starting to appear.

Moving slowly and painfully, for what seemed like hours, at last they reached an inn.

The Samaritan helped the injured man down.

"Do you have a room for this poor man?" he asked the innkeeper. "He's been badly beaten."

The innkeeper helped get the injured man inside and together they put him to bed.

By morning he was feeling much better, and the Samaritan had to be on his way.

"Look after my friend!" he told the innkeeper. "Take this money. Make sure he has all the food and medicine he needs. If it costs more, I'll pay when I come by again."

A question

"Now," Jesus asked his listeners, "who can tell me which of the three men – the priest, the Temple helper, or the Samaritan – acted like a good friend to the man who was robbed?"

"The man who helped," came the answer. "The Samaritan."

"Of course," said Jesus. "Now go and do the same!"

Luke 10:25–37

The Lost Sheep

HERE IS ANOTHER of the much-loved stories Jesus told.

There was once a good shepherd.

He had exactly one hundred sheep. He knew them all by name, and loved every one of them.

Each morning the shepherd counted his sheep. One, two, three, four... 97, 98, 99, 100.

Each day the shepherd took his sheep to green fields, and found them a stream to drink from.

The shepherd guarded his sheep carefully, scaring away wolves and bears.

Each night the shepherd led his sheep back to their fold. Then the shepherd counted his sheep again. One, two, three, four... 97, 98, 99, 100.

When all the sheep were safe inside, the shepherd shut the gate.

In the morning, the shepherd counted his sheep all over again. Then he led them out to find fresh grass and cool water.

Missing!

One night the shepherd was counting his sheep as usual. One, two, three, four... 97, 98, 99 – only 99!

Oh no! He must have missed one.

The shepherd began to count again. One, two, three, four... 97, 98, 99... Now the shepherd was worried.

"One sheep is missing!" he said. "I must go and find it."

So the shepherd shut the ninety-nine sheep safe inside their fold. Then he set out to search for his lost sheep.

The shepherd splashed across a stream and clambered over rocks.

He climbed a hill and slithered down the other side. But he found no sheep.

"Where are you, lost sheep?" called the shepherd.

In the distance, he heard a wolf howl.

He walked for miles and miles. It was dark and cold, and he felt tired and hungry.

The shepherd searched all the places where his sheep might have strayed.

The shepherd stopped and listened. "*Baa*."

He listened again.

The shepherd walked towards the "*baa*".

It had to be his lost sheep!

It was! The lost sheep had got caught in a spiky, prickly bush.

The shepherd gently pulled his sheep from the bush. The little sheep's coat was badly torn, and it was bleeding from some cuts.

At last the shepherd had found the lost sheep. He carried it home on his strong shoulders. How happy he was!

The shepherd called to his friends. "Be happy!" he said. "I have found my lost sheep."

Jesus said, "I am like a good shepherd. I care for people who are lost."
Luke 15:1–7

The Boy Who Came Home

JESUS ALSO TOLD this great story.

There was once a rich farmer. He had a beautiful house, a huge farm, many servants, great flocks of sheep, and vast herds of cows. And best of all he had two sons.

"Dad has lots of money," the younger son thought to himself one day. "When he dies, I'll get my share. But I'll ask him to give me my share *now*. Then I can set off on a big adventure."

So the younger son went to his father. "Dad," he said. "You've got lots of money. I don't want to wait years to get my share. Give me my money now, then I can go off and enjoy myself."

The father felt sad. He loved having his son at home.

But he gave the younger son his share of the money, as he asked.

had a wonderful time!

Then one day his money ran out. And when the money went, his friends vanished too.

No more parties! No friends! No work! No money! What was he to do?

"I'll have to find work and earn some more money," he said to himself. "Otherwise I'll starve."

Stupid!

But it wasn't easy to find work. And to make things worse, famine came – and there wasn't much food for anyone.

So the younger son went to a farmer.

"I'm terribly hungry," he told the farmer. "Give me something to eat. I'll work really hard for you."

"You can look after my pigs," said the farmer.

So the boy sat under a tree, minding the grunting, greedy pigs.

"I'm so hungry, I could eat the disgusting food I'm throwing to these mucky pigs," he thought to himself.

Before long the boy started thinking of his family back home.

"How stupid I've been!" he said to himself. "Lots of men work for my father. They get as much food as they need. And here am I, with an empty tummy, envying the pigs their food!"

He also remembered how kind his father had always been.

"I know what I'll do!" he said to himself.

A big adventure

This son felt very pleased with himself.

That very day he packed his bags and left home, thinking of all the money in his pockets. What a great time he would have!

His dad was sad to see his son leave home. Each morning he climbed onto the roof of his house. Perhaps he would see his boy coming back home today…

But his son kept walking for days, until he reached a big city in a far country. There he bought himself a house.

As soon as people knew he had lots of money, they flocked around him. The younger son gave lots of parties.

It was great! He could eat and drink with his new friends from morning to night. He

"I'll go home and say, 'Father, I've done wrong in God's sight – and in yours too. I don't deserve to be called your son any more. But can I work for you and earn enough to pay for my food?'"

So he set off on the long walk home.

The boy walked for miles. He was dirty and tired, and his clothes were in rags.

But the father had never forgotten his younger son. Every day still he climbed to the roof of his house to see if his boy was coming home.

On this particular day, the father was watching as usual. Far in the distance, he spied a tiny figure. Surely that poor, ragged man wasn't his dear son?

A fantastic welcome

"It *is* my son," cried the old man.

And while the boy was still a long way off, the happy father ran to meet him. He hugged and kissed his son.

The boy started to speak the words he'd been practising all the way home.

"Dad, I'm so sorry… I don't deserve to be called your son… Can I work as one of your servants?…"

But his father just started to laugh. He wouldn't let his son say another word.

"My son is home again!" he shouted to his servants. "Quick – bring out the best clothes and put them on him. Slip a fine gold ring on his finger. Bring smart shoes for his feet! Cook a fantastic banquet! We must all celebrate.

"I thought my son was dead – but he's come back home. He was lost – now he's found. We're going to have such a party!"

The boy was nearly in tears. How could he ever have been so stupid as to leave his home and family? Jesus said, "In the same way, God is happy when he welcomes home people who are lost."
Luke 15:11–32

The Two House-Builders

JESUS ALSO TOLD this story.

Once two men each decided to build a house. The first man found a sandy place, with a stream gurgling past.

"This is a great place to build my house!" he said.

So he started to build his house on the sand.

He was in such a rush, he didn't dig any foundations.

He quickly built the walls, and put on a roof. His house was soon finished.

The second man searched really carefully for the best place to build his house. At last he found some hard rock that would suit well. He dug into the rock. Then he was ready to start building his house on firm foundations.

The walls of his house grew tall. At last the house on the rock was finished.

Almost at once black clouds appeared. Rain fell, winds blew, lightning flashed, and thunder roared.

The two men rushed into their houses.

Then CRRRAASHH!!! The first man's house fell flat! The man who built on the sand was left with nothing but a pile of stones!

But in spite of all the rain, the second man's house stood firm on the rock.

Jesus said, "People who listen to what I say are like the wise man who built his house on rock."

Luke 6:46–49

The Man in the Tree

THERE LIVED IN the city of Jericho a man named Zacchaeus.

He was the chief tax collector. Anyone who came to Jericho and wanted to sell things had to pay Zacchaeus tax money.

Zacchaeus grew very rich. He took more money than he was supposed to. People couldn't do anything about it.

"Zacchaeus is rich because he takes too much money from us," people said. "He's a thief!"

Nobody liked him.

One day people heard that Jesus was going to visit the city of Jericho.

Everyone crowded into the streets to try to see him. They'd heard about the wonderful stories Jesus told and the healing miracles he did.

Zacchaeus the tax collector wanted to see Jesus too.

But Zacchaeus was very, very short.

He didn't have a chance of seeing anything if he was at the back of a crowd. And nobody in Jericho was going to let Zacchaeus stand at the front of the crowd because they disliked him so much.

Come down!

Just then, Zacchaeus had a brainwave!

Quickly, he ran ahead of the crowds. He clambered up a sycamore tree and perched on a high branch. Now he would be able to see Jesus when he passed by! And no one would notice him, hidden up in the sycamore tree!

Soon the crowds came along. There were Jesus' friends – and there was Jesus!

Then Zacchaeus got a big shock. Jesus reached his tree and stopped. He looked up.

"Zacchaeus," Jesus called, "come down!"

Zacchaeus blushed.

"I'm coming to dinner in your home today!" said Jesus.

Zacchaeus was astonished.

Never before had something so extraordinary happened to him.

He slithered down the tree, nearly falling from its branches in his haste.

Dinner with Zacchaeus

Zacchaeus walked to his house with Jesus, and they had dinner.

Zacchaeus was so happy that Jesus had come to visit him.

But the people of Jericho were furious.

"Zacchaeus is a bad person," they complained. "He's a thief! Jesus shouldn't be visiting such a horrible, greedy man!"

But after he met with Jesus, Zacchaeus changed completely.

He was much nicer. Much kinder.

"I've taken too much money from everyone," he said. "Now I want to put things right."

"I've decided: I'm going to give half my money to poor people," Zacchaeus said. "And I'm going to give back twice as much money to the people I stole from! I'm going to put right all the wrong things I've done."

"Today is a very special day for you, Zacchaeus," said Jesus.

"God is very pleased that you're making a fresh start."

Luke 19:1–10

Jesus Rides into Jerusalem

IT WAS THE TIME of the great Jewish festival called Passover.

Jesus decided to go to Jerusalem for the feast with his special friends, the twelve disciples.

On the way to the city Jesus told them, "I'm going to be taken prisoner and killed in Jerusalem. But after three days, I will rise from the dead."

The disciples didn't understand what he was talking about.

When they arrived near a village called Bethany, just outside Jerusalem, Jesus sent off two of his friends.

"Go into the next village," he told them. "You'll find a donkey tied up. No one has ever ridden it. Untie the donkey and bring it to me. If anyone asks what you're doing, just say, 'The master needs the donkey!'"

The two disciples found the donkey quite easily, just as Jesus had told them.

They untied it and brought it to Jesus. Some of Jesus' friends spread their cloaks over the donkey's back.

Hooray for God!

Then Jesus sat on the young donkey and rode into Jerusalem. The road was full of people going to the city for the great festival.

When the crowds saw Jesus coming, they grew very excited. Some welcomed Jesus as their king, spreading their cloaks on the ground before him.

Others cut branches from palm trees and laid them down on the road.

Some people began to shout with joy.

Soon everyone joined in, chanting, "Hosanna! Hooray for God!" and "Praise God in heaven!"

But some of the priests from the Temple hated Jesus. They were plotting to kill him.

One of Jesus' disciples, a man named Judas Iscariot, went to the chief priests.

"If you pay me well," said Judas, "I can show you where you will find Jesus and capture him easily."

The priests were delighted.

They promised to pay Judas thirty silver coins for doing this.

Judas waited for a good moment to hand Jesus over to them.

Jesus gets cross

When they arrived in Jerusalem, Jesus and his disciples went to the Temple.

Jesus saw many shopkeepers had set up tables there, and were selling goods and changing money.

He was very angry.

"You've made God's Temple into a den of thieves!" he shouted at them.

Then Jesus chased the men who were buying and selling right out of the Temple.

He threw over their tables and overturned their stalls.

"My Temple should be a house of prayer for all the nations of the world," said Jesus.
Luke 19:28–48

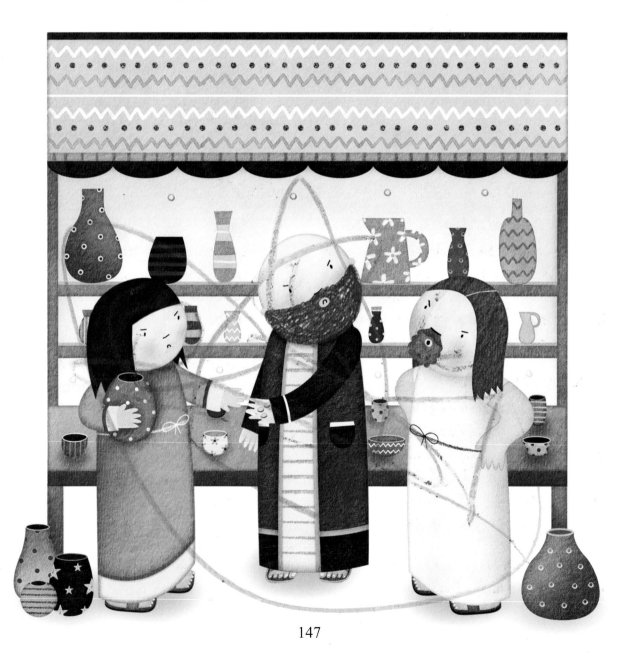

147

A Special Meal

THE DAY ARRIVED for the great feast of Passover. At Passover, Jewish families cook lamb for dinner in their home.

Jesus wanted to celebrate Passover with his twelve special friends.

They gathered for the meal in an upstairs room in Jerusalem.

As they ate together, Jesus said to his friends, "Love one another, just as I have loved you."

Then he said suddenly, "One of you eating this meal with me is going to hand me over to my enemies."

The disciples were frightened.

"Jesus, you can't mean me!" they all said.

"I'm talking about the person who is dipping into the same bowl as I am," said Jesus.

"Surely you don't mean me," said Judas.

"Yes – it's you," said Jesus.

Then Judas crept out.

He was plotting against Jesus.

Bread and wine

Jesus took some bread.

He thanked God for it, broke it, and gave a piece to each of his friends.

After this Jesus said, "Take this bread and eat it! *I* am the bread. I am giving myself for you all."

Then Jesus took a cup of wine.
He thanked God for it.

Jesus passed the cup to his friends, saying, "Drink some of this wine! The wine is my life. I offer my life for all."

So the disciples drank the wine.

At the end of the meal, they sang a hymn.

Jesus prays

After supper, Jesus took his disciples outside the city.

He led them to a garden called Gethsemane on the Mount of Olives.

"Wait for me here," said Jesus. "I want to pray alone. Stay awake – and pray too!"

Then Jesus chose three of his special friends – Peter, James, and John – to pray with him.

He told these three, "I feel so very sad. Please stay here and pray."

Then Jesus went a little further and knelt to pray. He was worried about what was going to happen.

"Father, don't make me have to do this!" he prayed. "But it's not what I want – it's what you want."

Jesus walked back to find the three disciples.

They were all fast asleep.

"Peter!" Jesus said, waking him up. "Why are you sleeping? Couldn't you pray for just one hour? Watch – and pray!"

Then Jesus went off alone into the garden again to pray.

But the disciples went back to sleep.

Jesus is betrayed

Later, Jesus came back.

"Wake up!" he said to his friends. "Look – here comes the man who is going to hand me over to my enemies!"

And there was Judas, leading men with swords and sticks.

Judas had agreed a secret sign with the priests. He had told them, "The man I kiss is the one you must arrest."

Judas walked straight up to Jesus and kissed him.

Then he said, "Teacher!"

So the men with Judas knew this was Jesus.

The soldiers grabbed Jesus and took him prisoner.

Now the disciples felt very frightened.

They all ran off and left Jesus alone.

Matthew 26:17–56

The Very First Easter

THE SOLDIERS MARCHED Jesus off to the high priest, who had called together the other priests.

They said Jesus had done wrong. They wanted to have him put to death.

"Are you the king whom God has sent?" the high priest asked Jesus. "Are you the Son of God?"

"Yes," Jesus answered, "I am."

"Did you hear that?" the high priests shouted angrily. "He says he's the Son of God!"

Next morning the priests took Jesus to the Roman ruler, Pilate.

"This man Jesus is making a lot of trouble," the priests told Pilate. "You should have him put to death!"

Pilate questioned Jesus carefully.

"I can find nothing wrong with him," said Pilate, when he had finished.

Then Pilate asked Jesus, "Are you the king of the Jews?"

"Yes, it is as you say," Jesus answered.

Pilate turned to the crowd of people who had gathered to watch.

"What shall I do with this king of the Jews? Shall I let him go free?" he asked.

But the noisy crowd all shouted, "To the cross with him! To the cross!"

So Pilate said, "Then I will send him to die on a cross."

Cruel soldiers

Now cruel Roman soldiers started to make fun of Jesus.

They stuck a crown made of spiky thorns on his head, as if he were a king.

They mocked him and pretended to salute him.

"Long live the king!" they shouted.

Then they hit him and spat at him.

Finally Roman soldiers marched Jesus out through the gates of Jerusalem, to a hill outside the city.

There they fixed him on a wooden cross. They also put two robbers on crosses, one on Jesus' right and the other on Jesus' left.

People passing by made fun of Jesus.

But Jesus said, "Father God, forgive these people!"

One of the robbers asked Jesus, "Please remember me!"

Jesus said to the robber, "Today you will be with me in heaven."

At midday the sky went dark.

Then Jesus died.

A Roman captain who was standing there said, "This really was God's Son!"

Jesus' family and friends stood and watched sadly.

Jesus is buried

After Jesus died on the cross, a good man named Joseph went to Pilate.

"Jesus has died," he said. "May I look after his body?"

The Roman ruler Pilate nodded, "Yes, you may!"

So Joseph took Jesus' body from the cross. He wrapped it in a linen cloth, and laid it in a grave carved out of rock.

Finally, Joseph rolled a huge stone across the doorway of the grave, so Jesus' body would be safe and undisturbed.

Two Roman soldiers guarded the door.
Mark 14:53-62, 15:1–47

Jesus is Alive!

EARLY ON SUNDAY MORNING, while it was still dark, Jesus' friend Mary Magdalene went to his tomb. She was carrying perfume to put on Jesus' body.

When she arrived, Mary was astonished to see that the big stone in front of the door had been rolled back.

But she couldn't see Jesus' body.

Mary dashed off back into Jerusalem. She wanted to tell Peter and John what she had found.

"They've taken away Jesus' body," she cried. "I can't find it!"

Peter and John were concerned. They decided to go to see for themselves, and rushed off to the tomb.

John arrived first, because he could run faster than Peter. As soon as he arrived, John bent down at the door of the tomb and peered in.

When Peter arrived, all out of breath, he dashed straight into the tomb. There was no body. The sheets that Jesus' body had been wrapped in were neatly folded.

Suddenly an angel appeared.

"Jesus isn't here," said the angel. "He is alive!"

Immediately Peter and John believed that Jesus had come back from the dead.

Jesus appears to Mary

Peter and John went back into Jerusalem.

But Mary Magdalene stayed outside the tomb, crying. She peered into the tomb.

Through her tears, Mary saw two angels dressed in white.

"Why are you crying?" they asked Mary.

"They've taken Jesus' body away," Mary

answered. "I don't know where it is."

Then Mary turned round and saw Jesus standing there – but she didn't know it was him.

"Why are you crying?" Jesus asked Mary. "Who are you looking for?"

Mary thought it was the gardener, so she said, "If you've taken Jesus' body, please tell me where you've put it."

Then Jesus said, "Mary!"

Immediately Mary knew he was Jesus.

"*Teacher!*" she said.

Mary dashed away to find the disciples.

"I've seen Jesus," she told them.

"He's alive!"

John 20:1–18

Supper with Jesus

AFTER JESUS HAD DIED, two of his followers were walking to Emmaus, a village outside Jerusalem.

They had heard some of Jesus' friends say they had seen Jesus alive again. But they felt sad, because they still thought Jesus was dead.

As they walked, the two men talked about everything that had happened in Jerusalem in the last few days. They remembered how Jesus had been arrested and taken before Pilate. And how Jesus had died on a cross.

Suddenly a stranger appeared on the road and started to walk with them. It was Jesus – but the men didn't recognize him.

"What are you talking about?" Jesus asked. They stopped in surprise.

One of them, named Cleopas, answered, "You must be the only visitor to Jerusalem who doesn't know what happened there."

"What?" asked Jesus.

"All the things they did to Jesus of Nazareth," they said. "The priests handed him over to Pilate so that Jesus could be put to death. Then some women shocked us saying they couldn't find Jesus' body when they visited his tomb this morning."

"God wanted everything to happen this way," Jesus explained to them. "Why don't you believe what these women told you?"

A guest to supper

They were now close to Emmaus, but the men thought the stranger was going further.

"Stay with us," they said to him. "It's already evening; soon it will be dark."

So Jesus stayed and sat down to supper with them.

He took some bread, and thanked God for the food. Then Jesus broke the loaf and gave each of the men some bread.

Suddenly the men saw that the stranger was Jesus!

At that moment, he disappeared.

"That was Jesus!" said Cleopas. "Didn't you feel excited when he was explaining things to us, as we walked with him?"

They jumped up, left the meal, and rushed back to Jerusalem.

They soon found Jesus' disciples.

"It's all true!" they told them. "Jesus really is alive! We've seen him with our own eyes!"

Luke 24:13–35

Jesus Returns to His Father

FORTY DAYS AFTER EASTER, Jesus' special friends, the disciples, were all together in a house in Jerusalem.

Suddenly Jesus appeared in the middle of the room.

At first they were all quite frightened.

to the Mount of Olives, just outside Jerusalem.

While they were standing with him on the hill, Jesus said to them, "Now I'm going to be with God. But I am still *always* with you. I will always be with you."

Jesus goes away

Then, as Jesus was still talking to them, a cloud came down from the sky.

It took Jesus away.

When the cloud disappeared, the disciples couldn't see Jesus any more.

They stood staring up into the sky, hoping to see Jesus again.

Suddenly two angels appeared. "Why are you all standing here staring up into the sky?" asked the angels. "Jesus is now with God in heaven. One day he will return. Just do what Jesus told you to do."

But Jesus said calmly, "Don't be afraid! Men killed me – but God has brought me back to life."

The disciples asked, "Will you become the king of the world now?"

"No – not yet," said Jesus. "A lot has to happen first. I want you to go into every country in the world. You must tell everyone that God loves them. Tell them about me. You shall be my messengers."

After this Jesus walked with his disciples

So the disciples walked back into Jerusalem. They went to the Temple and thanked God for everything that had happened.
Acts 1:9–12